Contents

Rider Information

Name:	Age:	DOB:
Home Address:		
Phone:	Email:	
Medical Conditions and Issues (Asthma, Allergies, etc.):		
Current Medications:		

Emergency Contact Name:	
Phone:	Mobile:
Email:	

Barn Name:
Contact Information:

"In riding a horse, we borrow freedom."
HELEN THOMPSON

Contact List

"The horse, with beauty unsurpassed, strength immeasurable
and grace unlike any other, still remains humble enough
to carry a man upon his back."

AMBER SENTI

Name	Address	Email	Phone

Name	Address	Email	Phone

Expenses

"Bread may feed my body, but my horse feeds my soul."

Monthly Riding Expense Worksheet

DATE: _____

Board	
Lease Payment	
Insurance	
Lessons	
Training Fees	
Veterinarian	
Farrier	
Horse Medications	
Supplements	
Treats	
Tack and Equipment Purchases	
Tack and Equipment Repairs	
Riding Apparel Purchase	
Association Membership Fees	
Show Entry Fees	
Trailering	
Coaching Fees	
Gas	
Car Repair	
Other Expenses	
TOTAL EXPENSES	

Monthly Riding Expense Worksheet

DATE: _____

Board	
Lease Payment	
Insurance	
Lessons	
Training Fees	
Veterinarian	
Farrier	
Horse Medications	
Supplements	
Treats	
Tack and Equipment Purchases	
Tack and Equipment Repairs	
Riding Apparel Purchase	
Association Membership Fees	
Show Entry Fees	
Trailering	
Coaching Fees	
Gas	
Car Repair	
Other Expenses	
TOTAL EXPENSES	

Monthly Riding Expense Worksheet

DATE: _____

Board	
Lease Payment	
Insurance	
Lessons	
Training Fees	
Veterinarian	
Farrier	
Horse Medications	
Supplements	
Treats	
Tack and Equipment Purchases	
Tack and Equipment Repairs	
Riding Apparel Purchase	
Association Membership Fees	
Show Entry Fees	
Trailering	
Coaching Fees	
Gas	
Car Repair	
Other Expenses	
TOTAL EXPENSES	

Monthly Riding Expense Worksheet

DATE: _____

Board	
Lease Payment	
Insurance	
Lessons	
Training Fees	
Veterinarian	
Farrier	
Horse Medications	
Supplements	
Treats	
Tack and Equipment Purchases	
Tack and Equipment Repairs	
Riding Apparel Purchase	
Association Membership Fees	
Show Entry Fees	
Trailering	
Coaching Fees	
Gas	
Car Repair	
Other Expenses	
TOTAL EXPENSES	

Monthly Riding Expense Worksheet

DATE: _____

Board	
Lease Payment	
Insurance	
Lessons	
Training Fees	
Veterinarian	
Farrier	
Horse Medications	
Supplements	
Treats	
Tack and Equipment Purchases	
Tack and Equipment Repairs	
Riding Apparel Purchase	
Association Membership Fees	
Show Entry Fees	
Trailering	
Coaching Fees	
Gas	
Car Repair	
Other Expenses	
TOTAL EXPENSES	

Monthly Riding Expense Worksheet

DATE: _____

Board	
Lease Payment	
Insurance	
Lessons	
Training Fees	
Veterinarian	
Farrier	
Horse Medications	
Supplements	
Treats	
Tack and Equipment Purchases	
Tack and Equipment Repairs	
Riding Apparel Purchase	
Association Membership Fees	
Show Entry Fees	
Trailering	
Coaching Fees	
Gas	
Car Repair	
Other Expenses	
TOTAL EXPENSES	

Monthly Riding Expense Worksheet

DATE: _____

Board	
Lease Payment	
Insurance	
Lessons	
Training Fees	
Veterinarian	
Farrier	
Horse Medications	
Supplements	
Treats	
Tack and Equipment Purchases	
Tack and Equipment Repairs	
Riding Apparel Purchase	
Association Membership Fees	
Show Entry Fees	
Trailering	
Coaching Fees	
Gas	
Car Repair	
Other Expenses	
TOTAL EXPENSES	

Monthly Riding Expense Worksheet

DATE: _____

Board	
Lease Payment	
Insurance	
Lessons	
Training Fees	
Veterinarian	
Farrier	
Horse Medications	
Supplements	
Treats	
Tack and Equipment Purchases	
Tack and Equipment Repairs	
Riding Apparel Purchase	
Association Membership Fees	
Show Entry Fees	
Trailering	
Coaching Fees	
Gas	
Car Repair	
Other Expenses	
TOTAL EXPENSES	

Monthly Riding Expense Worksheet

DATE: _____

Board	
Lease Payment	
Insurance	
Lessons	
Training Fees	
Veterinarian	
Farrier	
Horse Medications	
Supplements	
Treats	
Tack and Equipment Purchases	
Tack and Equipment Repairs	
Riding Apparel Purchase	
Association Membership Fees	
Show Entry Fees	
Trailering	
Coaching Fees	
Gas	
Car Repair	
Other Expenses	
TOTAL EXPENSES	

Monthly Riding Expense Worksheet

DATE: _____

Board	
Lease Payment	
Insurance	
Lessons	
Training Fees	
Veterinarian	
Farrier	
Horse Medications	
Supplements	
Treats	
Tack and Equipment Purchases	
Tack and Equipment Repairs	
Riding Apparel Purchase	
Association Membership Fees	
Show Entry Fees	
Trailering	
Coaching Fees	
Gas	
Car Repair	
Other Expenses	
TOTAL EXPENSES	

Saddle Fitting and Adjustment Record

Date	Type	Fitter/Saddle Maker	Cost

Blanket Washing and Repair Record

Date	Type of Service	Service Person/Company	Cost

Tack and Equipment Repair Record

Date	Type of Service	Repair Person	Cost

Tack and Equipment Repair Record

Date	Type of Service	Repair Person	Cost

Health & Wellness

"Horses change lives. They give our young people confidence and self-esteem. They provide peace and tranquility to troubled souls. They give us hope!"

TONI ROBINSON

Personal Wellness Information

Describe your usual state of wellness to use as a baseline and discover what wellness factors might be impacting your riding.

Eating Habits: Poor   Fair   Average   Good   Great

Water Intake: <2   2-4   4-6   6-8   >8
(in 8oz glasses per day)

Medications, Vitamins, Herbal Supplements

Description	Dosage	Purpose

Alcoholic Drinks Per Week: _____   Cigarettes Per Day: _____

Hours of Sleep per Night: <4   4-6   6-8   >8

Pain and Discomfort

Location	Cause	Current Treatment

Daily Stress Levels: Extreme   High   Medium   Low

Stress Management Techniques: _____

_____

_____

Exercise Other Than Riding:

<20 min./day, 3 days/wk   20 min./day, 3 days/wk   >20min./day, 3 days/wk

Injury Record

Injury	Date	Recommended Treatment	Recommended Time Off

If I'm injured, I can modify my riding by: _____

_____

_____

_____

If I can't ride, I can keep up my skills by: _____

_____

_____

_____

_____

Personal Mindfulness Baseline

Answer the following prompts to help you express how you feel about your riding at this moment. This will give you a baseline to look back on as your riding progresses over the year.

I ride because: _____

_____

_____

_____

My riding goal for the year is: _____

_____

_____

■ I can achieve that goal by doing the following things: _____

_____

_____

_____

My favourite part of riding is _____ because: _____

_____

_____

_____

The most stressful part of riding is _____ because: _____

_____

_____

_____

■ I do the following things to manage that stress: _____

_____

_____

_____

_____

My biggest success as a rider is: _____

_____

■ I want to build on that success in order to: _____

_____

_____

_____

My biggest obstacle as a rider is: _____

_____

■ This is my plan to overcome that obstacle: _____

_____

_____

My best habit as a rider is: _____

_____

■ I will use that habit to: _____

_____

_____

_____

My worst habit as a rider is: _____

_____

■ I will change that habit by committing to doing the following: _____

_____

_____

_____

_____

Riding Journal

"You can see what man made from the seat of an automobile, but the best way to see what God made is from the back of a horse."

CHARLES M. RUSSELL

The quality of our riding depends on us bringing the best of our whole selves to the saddle every day. These pages will ask you to jot down your daily riding goals and your riding experiences. They will also challenge you to think about how other factors might be influencing your riding. You can use the icons to identify:

Whether you met (or are likely to meet) your exercise goals for the day:

| Started | Working on it | Met Goals |

If you were well rested (How many hours of sleep you had the night before):

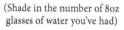 1   2   3   4   5   6   7   8+

| If you were hydrated at the beginning of your ride: (Shade in the number of 8oz glasses of water you've had) | How stressed you were when you started your ride: (Shade in where you think your stress levels are at) |

Whether your body was fueled on healthy foods:

| Did Not Eat Well | Half-Way | Fully Fueled |

The icons are only here to help you think about your riding holistically. There's no gold standard, and no pressure. If they're not helpful, skip them! If you don't reach your goals, that's ok. Be gentle with yourself. Every day is a new opportunity to take good care of yourself.

Prompts for contemplation will appear to guide you in your writing, but write about whatever you wish. If a prompt doesn't seem right in that moment, you can ignore it or keep it in the back of your mind to use on a different day (the prompts are also collected on a single page at the back of the section for reference).

Daily Riding Journal

Date: **7/2/18**

Stress

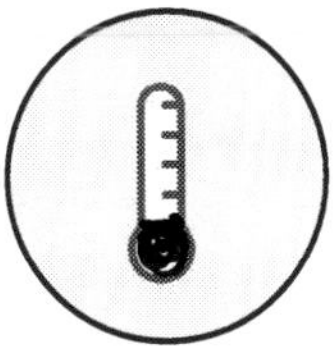

Exercise Goals

Sleep 1 2 3 4 5 6 (7) 8+

Hydration

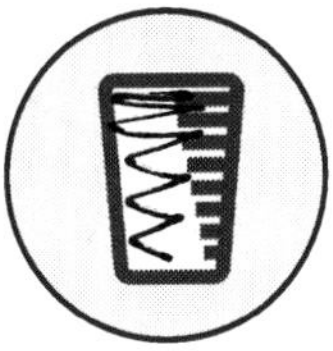

Healthy Eating

My riding goal for the day is: _To be good!_

My ride was: _good I rode Wellington._

Date: 7/3/18

Stress

Exercise Goals

Sleep   1   2   3   4   5   6   7   (8+)

Hydration

Healthy Eating

My riding goal for the day is: _to be good to be, able to_
Move up

My ride was: ~~good~~ The best because I rode
Blazer

34

Date: 7/4/18

Stress

Exercise Goals

Sleep   1   2   3   4   5   6   7 (8+)

Hydration

Healthy Eating

My riding goal for the day is: __be good in my new group__

My ride was: __good because I moved up & rode cool Mike and Mojo__

Date: _____

Stress

Exercise Goals

Sleep   1   2   3   4   5   6   7   8+

Hydration

Healthy Eating

My riding goal for the day is: _____

_____

_____

_____

_____

My ride was: _____

_____

_____

_____

_____

_____

_____

_____

Date: _____

Stress

Exercise Goals

Sleep   1   2   3   4   5   6   7   8+

Hydration

Healthy Eating

My riding goal for the day is:

_____

_____

_____

_____

My ride was: _____

_____

_____

_____

_____

_____

_____

Riding makes me feel: _____

_____

_____

_____

_____

_____

_____

_____

_____

_____

_____

_____

_____

Date: _____

Stress

Exercise Goals

Sleep   1   2   3   4   5   6   7   8+

Hydration

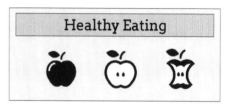

Healthy Eating

My riding goal for the day is: _____

_____

_____

_____

_____

My ride was: _____

_____

_____

_____

_____

_____

_____

_____

Date: _____

Stress

Exercise Goals

Sleep   1   2   3   4   5   6   7   8+

Hydration

Healthy Eating

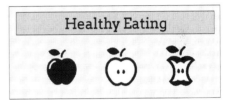

My riding goal for the day is: _____

_____

_____

_____

_____

My ride was: _____

_____

_____

_____

_____

_____

_____

_____

Date: _____

Stress

Exercise Goals

Sleep   1   2   3   4   5   6   7   8+

Hydration

Healthy Eating

My riding goal for the day is: _____

_____

_____

_____

_____

My ride was: _____

_____

_____

_____

_____

_____

_____

_____

Date: _____

Stress

Exercise Goals

Sleep   1   2   3   4   5   6   7   8+

Hydration

Healthy Eating

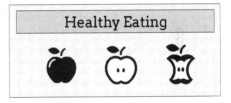

My riding goal for the day is:

_____

_____

_____

_____

My ride was: _____

_____

_____

_____

_____

_____

_____

Take a moment and describe the partnership you have with your horse.

_____

_____

_____

_____

_____

_____

_____

_____

_____

_____

_____

Date: _____

Stress

Exercise Goals

Sleep   1   2   3   4   5   6   7   8+

Hydration

Healthy Eating

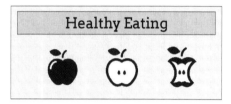

My riding goal for the day is: _____

_____

_____

_____

_____

My ride was: _____

_____

_____

_____

_____

_____

_____

_____

Date: _____

Stress

Exercise Goals

Sleep   1   2   3   4   5   6   7   8+

Hydration

Healthy Eating

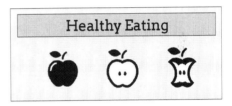

My riding goal for the day is: _____

_____

_____

_____

_____

My ride was: _____

_____

_____

_____

_____

_____

_____

Date:_____

Stress

Exercise Goals

Sleep   1   2   3   4   5   6   7   8+

Hydration

Healthy Eating

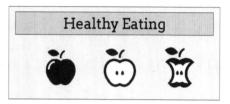

My riding goal for the day is: _____

_____

_____

_____

_____

My ride was: _____

_____

_____

_____

_____

_____

_____

_____

_____

Date: _____

Stress

Exercise Goals

Sleep   1   2   3   4   5   6   7   8+

Hydration

Healthy Eating

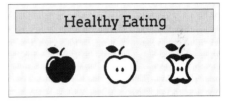

My riding goal for the day is:

_____

_____

_____

_____

My ride was: _____

_____

_____

_____

_____

_____

_____

How can you be more present for your horse when you ride?

_____

_____

_____

_____

_____

_____

_____

_____

_____

Date: _____

Stress

Sleep   1 2 3 4 5 6 7 8+

Hydration

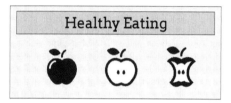

My riding goal for the day is: _____

_____

_____

_____

_____

My ride was: _____

_____

_____

_____

_____

_____

_____

_____

_____

Date: _____

Stress

Exercise Goals

Sleep   1 2 3 4 5 6 7 8+

Hydration

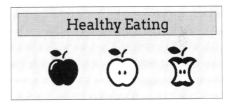

Healthy Eating

My riding goal for the day is: _____

_____

_____

_____

_____

My ride was: _____

_____

_____

_____

_____

_____

_____

_____

Date: _____

Stress

Exercise Goals

Sleep   1   2   3   4   5   6   7   8+

Hydration

Healthy Eating

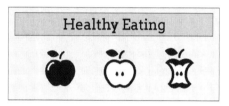

My riding goal for the day is: _____

_____

_____

_____

_____

My ride was: _____

_____

_____

_____

_____

_____

_____

Date: _____

Stress

Exercise Goals

Sleep   1   2   3   4   5   6   7   8+

Hydration

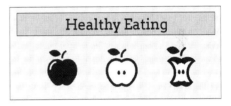

Healthy Eating

My riding goal for the day is:

_____

_____

_____

_____

My ride was: _____

_____

_____

_____

_____

_____

_____

_____

I feel most alive when I'm:

_____

_____

_____

_____

_____

_____

_____

_____

_____

_____

_____

_____

Date: _____

Stress

Sleep   1   2   3   4   5   6   7   8+

Hydration

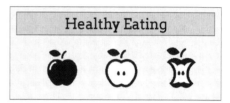

My riding goal for the day is: _____

_____

_____

_____

_____

My ride was: _____

_____

_____

_____

_____

_____

_____

_____

Date: _____

Stress

Exercise Goals

Sleep 1　2　3　4　5　6　7　8+

Hydration

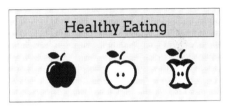

Healthy Eating

My riding goal for the day is: _____

_____

_____

_____

_____

My ride was: _____

_____

_____

_____

_____

_____

_____

Date: _____

Stress

Exercise Goals

Sleep 1 2 3 4 5 6 7 8+

Hydration

Healthy Eating

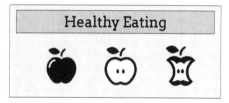

My riding goal for the day is: _____

_____

_____

_____

_____

My ride was: _____

_____

_____

_____

_____

_____

_____

_____

Date: _____

Stress

Exercise Goals

Sleep   1   2   3   4   5   6   7   8+

Hydration

Healthy Eating

My riding goal for the day is:

_____

_____

_____

_____

My ride was: _____

_____

_____

_____

_____

_____

_____

Today I was challenged by:

Date: _____

Stress

Exercise Goals

Sleep   1 2 3 4 5 6 7 8+

Hydration

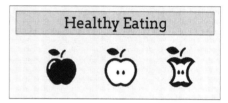

Healthy Eating

My riding goal for the day is: _____

_____

_____

_____

_____

My ride was: _____

_____

_____

_____

_____

_____

_____

_____

Date: _____

Stress

Exercise Goals

Sleep 1 2 3 4 5 6 7 8+

Hydration

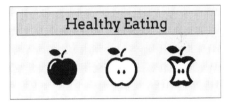
Healthy Eating

My riding goal for the day is: _____

_____

_____

_____

_____

My ride was: _____

_____

_____

_____

_____

_____

_____

Date: _____

Stress

Sleep   1   2   3   4   5   6   7   8+

Hydration

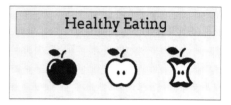

My riding goal for the day is: _____

_____

_____

_____

_____

My ride was: _____

_____

_____

_____

_____

_____

_____

_____

Date: _____

Stress

Exercise Goals

Sleep   1 2 3 4 5 6 7 8+

Hydration

Healthy Eating

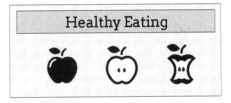

My riding goal for the day is:

_____

_____

_____

_____

My ride was: _____

_____

_____

_____

_____

_____

When my horse and I are really connected, it feels:

_____

_____

_____

_____

_____

_____

_____

_____

_____

_____

Date:_____

Stress

Exercise Goals

Sleep   1   2   3   4   5   6   7   8+

Hydration

Healthy Eating

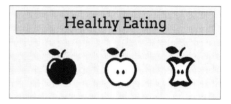

My riding goal for the day is: _____

_____

_____

_____

_____

My ride was: _____

_____

_____

_____

_____

_____

_____

_____

_____

Date: _____

Stress

Exercise Goals

Sleep   1   2   3   4   5   6   7   8+

Hydration

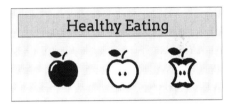

Healthy Eating

My riding goal for the day is: _____

_____

_____

_____

_____

My ride was: _____

_____

_____

_____

_____

_____

_____

Date:_____

Stress

Exercise Goals

Sleep   1   2   3   4   5   6   7   8+

Hydration

Healthy Eating

My riding goal for the day is: _____

_____

_____

_____

_____

My ride was: _____

_____

_____

_____

_____

_____

_____

_____

Date: _____

Stress

Exercise Goals

Sleep   1   2   3   4   5   6   7   8+

Hydration

Healthy Eating

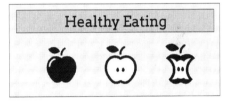

My riding goal for the day is:

_____

_____

_____

_____

My ride was: _____

_____

_____

_____

_____

_____

My horse and I are most together when:

_____

_____

_____

_____

_____

_____

_____

_____

_____

Date:_____

Stress

Exercise Goals

Sleep   1   2   3   4   5   6   7   8+

Hydration

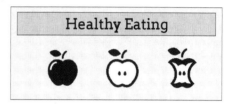
Healthy Eating

My riding goal for the day is: _____

_____

_____

_____

_____

My ride was: _____

_____

_____

_____

_____

_____

_____

_____

Date: _____

Stress

Exercise Goals

Sleep 1 2 3 4 5 6 7 8+

Hydration

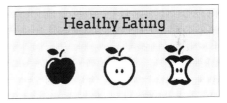
Healthy Eating

My riding goal for the day is: _____
_____
_____
_____
_____

My ride was: _____
_____
_____
_____
_____
_____
_____

Date:_____

Stress

Exercise Goals

Sleep   1   2   3   4   5   6   7   8+

Hydration

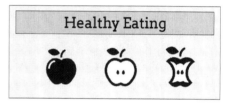

Healthy Eating

My riding goal for the day is: _____

_____

_____

_____

_____

My ride was:_____

_____

_____

_____

_____

_____

_____

_____

Date: _____

Stress

Sleep   1 2 3 4 5 6 7 8+

Hydration

My riding goal for the day is:

_____

_____

_____

_____

My ride was: —————————

_____

_____

_____

_____

_____

_____

This is how I will banish
negative thoughts today:

_____

_____

_____

_____

_____

_____

_____

_____

_____

_____

Date: _____

Stress

Sleep   1   2   3   4   5   6   7   8+

Hydration

My riding goal for the day is: _____

_____

_____

_____

_____

My ride was: _____

_____

_____

_____

_____

_____

_____

_____

_____

Date: _____

Stress

Sleep   1   2   3   4   5   6   7   8+

Hydration

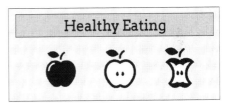

My riding goal for the day is: _____

_____

_____

_____

_____

My ride was: _____

_____

_____

_____

_____

_____

_____

Date: _____

Stress

Exercise Goals

Sleep   1   2   3   4   5   6   7   8+

Hydration

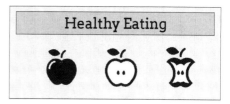

Healthy Eating

My riding goal for the day is: _____

_____

_____

_____

_____

My ride was: _____

_____

_____

_____

_____

_____

_____

_____

Date: _____

Stress

Exercise Goals

Sleep   1   2   3   4   5   6   7   8+

Hydration

Healthy Eating

My riding goal for the day is:

_____

_____

_____

_____

My ride was: _____

_____

_____

_____

_____

_____

_____

Take a moment and just breathe together with your horse. How does that affect your riding?

_____

_____

_____

_____

_____

_____

_____

_____

_____

Date: _____

Stress

Exercise Goals

Sleep   1   2   3   4   5   6   7   8+

Hydration

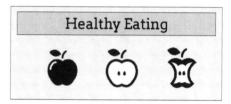
Healthy Eating

My riding goal for the day is: _____

_____

_____

_____

_____

My ride was: _____

_____

_____

_____

_____

_____

_____

_____

Date: _____

Stress

Exercise Goals

Sleep   1   2   3   4   5   6   7   8+

Hydration

Healthy Eating

My riding goal for the day is: _____

_____

_____

_____

_____

My ride was: _____

_____

_____

_____

_____

_____

_____

_____

Date:_____

Stress

Exercise Goals

Sleep   1   2   3   4   5   6   7   8+

Hydration

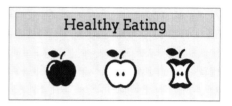

Healthy Eating

My riding goal for the day is: _____

_____

_____

_____

_____

My ride was: _____

_____

_____

_____

_____

_____

_____

_____

Date: _____

Stress

Exercise Goals

Sleep 　1　2　3　4　5　6　7　8+

Hydration

Healthy Eating

My riding goal for the day is:

_____

_____

_____

_____

My ride was: _____

_____

_____

_____

_____

_____

_____

I feel most at home in the saddle when I'm:

_____

_____

_____

_____

_____

_____

_____

_____

_____

_____

Date: _____

Stress

Exercise Goals

Sleep 1   2   3   4   5   6   7   8+

Hydration

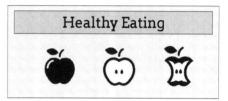

Healthy Eating

My riding goal for the day is: _____

_____

_____

_____

_____

My ride was: _____

_____

_____

_____

_____

_____

_____

_____

Date: _____

Stress

Sleep   1 2 3 4 5 6 7 8+

Hydration

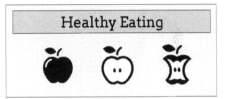

My riding goal for the day is: _____

_____

_____

_____

_____

My ride was: _____

_____

_____

_____

_____

_____

_____

_____

Date: _____

Stress

Exercise Goals

Sleep   1   2   3   4   5   6   7   8+

Hydration

Healthy Eating

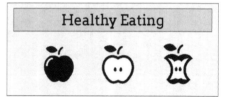

My riding goal for the day is: _____

_____

_____

_____

_____

My ride was: _____

_____

_____

_____

_____

_____

_____

_____

_____

Date: _____

Stress

Exercise Goals

Sleep 1 2 3 4 5 6 7 8+

Hydration

Healthy Eating

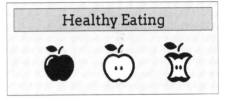

My riding goal for the day is:

_____

_____

_____

_____

My ride was: _____

_____

_____

_____

_____

_____

The strongest thing about my riding today was:

_____

_____

_____

_____

_____

_____

_____

_____

_____

_____

Date: _____

Stress

Sleep   1   2   3   4   5   6   7   8+

Hydration

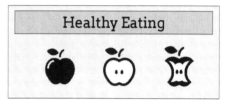

My riding goal for the day is: _____

_____

_____

_____

_____

My ride was: _____

_____

_____

_____

_____

_____

_____

_____

Date: _____

Stress

Exercise Goals

Sleep 1   2   3   4   5   6   7   8+

Hydration

Healthy Eating

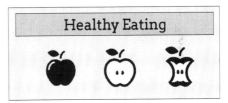

My riding goal for the day is: _____

_____

_____

_____

_____

My ride was: _____

_____

_____

_____

_____

_____

_____

Date:_____

Stress

Sleep   1   2   3   4   5   6   7   8+

Hydration

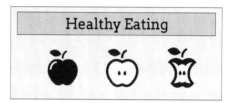

My riding goal for the day is: _____

_____

_____

_____

_____

My ride was: _____

_____

_____

_____

_____

_____

_____

_____

_____

Date: _____

Stress

Exercise Goals

Sleep

  1   2   3   4   5   6   7   8+

Hydration

Healthy Eating

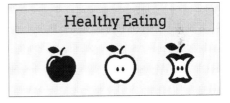

My riding goal for the day is:

_____

_____

_____

_____

My ride was: _____

_____

_____

_____

_____

_____

Today I will: _____

_____

_____

_____

_____

_____

_____

_____

_____

_____

_____

_____

_____

Date:_____

Stress

Sleep   1   2   3   4   5   6   7   8+

Hydration

My riding goal for the day is: _____

_____

_____

_____

_____

My ride was: _____

_____

_____

_____

_____

_____

_____

_____

Date: _____

Stress

Exercise Goals

Sleep 1   2   3   4   5   6   7   8+

Hydration

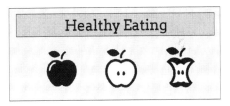

Healthy Eating

My riding goal for the day is: _____

_____

_____

_____

_____

My ride was: _____

_____

_____

_____

_____

_____

_____

_____

Date: _____

Stress

Sleep   1   2   3   4   5   6   7   8+

Hydration

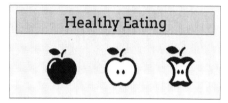

My riding goal for the day is: _____

_____

_____

_____

_____

My ride was: _____

_____

_____

_____

_____

_____

_____

_____

Date: _____

Stress

Exercise Goals

Sleep 1 2 3 4 5 6 7 8+

Hydration

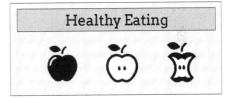

Healthy Eating

My riding goal for the day is:

_____

_____

_____

_____

My ride was: _____

_____

_____

_____

_____

_____

_____

This is what makes me trust in myself:

_____

_____

_____

_____

_____

_____

_____

_____

_____

_____

_____

Date: _____

Stress

Exercise Goals

Sleep   1   2   3   4   5   6   7   8+

Hydration

Healthy Eating

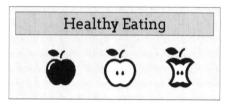

My riding goal for the day is: _____

_____

_____

_____

_____

My ride was: _____

_____

_____

_____

_____

_____

_____

_____

Date: _____

Stress

Exercise Goals

Sleep 1 2 3 4 5 6 7 8+

Hydration

Healthy Eating

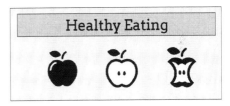

My riding goal for the day is: _____

_____

_____

_____

My ride was: _____

_____

_____

_____

_____

_____

_____

Date: _____

Stress

Exercise Goals

Sleep   1   2   3   4   5   6   7   8+

Hydration

Healthy Eating

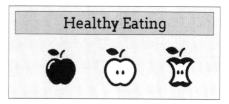

My riding goal for the day is: _____

_____

_____

_____

_____

My ride was: _____

_____

_____

_____

_____

_____

_____

Date: _____

Stress

Exercise Goals

Sleep   1   2   3   4   5   6   7   8+

Hydration

Healthy Eating

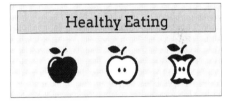

My riding goal for the day is:

_____

_____

_____

_____

My ride was: _____

_____

_____

_____

_____

_____

I love it when my horse: _____

_____

_____

_____

_____

_____

_____

_____

_____

_____

_____

Date: _____

Stress

Exercise Goals

Sleep   1   2   3   4   5   6   7   8+

Hydration

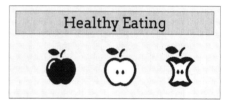

Healthy Eating

My riding goal for the day is: _____

_____

_____

_____

_____

My ride was: _____

_____

_____

_____

_____

_____

_____

_____

_____

Date: _____

Stress

Exercise Goals

Sleep   1   2   3   4   5   6   7   8+

Hydration

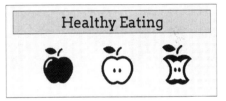

Healthy Eating

My riding goal for the day is: _____

_____

_____

_____

_____

My ride was: _____

_____

_____

_____

_____

_____

_____

_____

Date: _____

Stress

Sleep   1   2   3   4   5   6   7   8+

Hydration

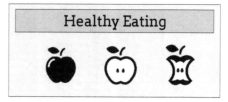

My riding goal for the day is: _____

_____

_____

_____

_____

My ride was: _____

_____

_____

_____

_____

_____

_____

_____

Date: _____

Stress

Exercise Goals

Sleep 1 2 3 4 5 6 7 8+

Hydration

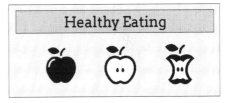
Healthy Eating

My riding goal for the day is:

_____

_____

_____

_____

My ride was: _____

_____

_____

_____

_____

_____

_____

What have you been avoiding in your riding? How will you confront it?

_____

_____

_____

_____

_____

_____

_____

_____

_____

_____

Date: _____

Stress

Exercise Goals

Sleep   1   2   3   4   5   6   7   8+

Hydration

Healthy Eating

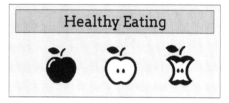

My riding goal for the day is: _____

_____

_____

_____

_____

My ride was: _____

_____

_____

_____

_____

_____

_____

_____

Date: _____

Stress

Exercise Goals

Sleep   1   2   3   4   5   6   7   8+

Hydration

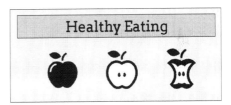
Healthy Eating

My riding goal for the day is: _____

_____

_____

_____

_____

My ride was: _____

_____

_____

_____

_____

_____

_____

Date: _____

Stress

Exercise Goals

Sleep   1   2   3   4   5   6   7   8+

Hydration

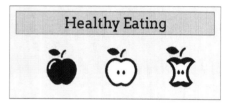
Healthy Eating

My riding goal for the day is: _____

_____

_____

_____

_____

My ride was: _____

_____

_____

_____

_____

_____

_____

_____

Date: _____

Stress

Exercise Goals

Sleep   1   2   3   4   5   6   7   8+

Hydration

Healthy Eating

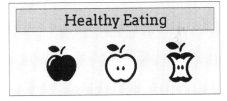

My riding goal for the day is:

_____

_____

_____

_____

My ride was: _____

_____

_____

_____

_____

_____

_____

I will work to stay open to new experiences by:

_____

_____

_____

_____

_____

_____

_____

_____

_____

_____

_____

Date: _____

Stress

Sleep   1   2   3   4   5   6   7   8+

Hydration

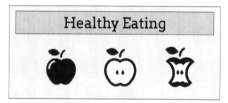

My riding goal for the day is: _____

_____

_____

_____

_____

My ride was: _____

_____

_____

_____

_____

_____

_____

_____

Date: _____

Stress

Exercise Goals

Sleep 1　2　3　4　5　6　7　8+

Hydration

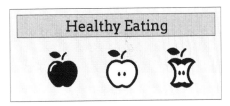

Healthy Eating

My riding goal for the day is: _____

_____

_____

_____

_____

My ride was: _____

_____

_____

_____

_____

_____

_____

Date: _____

Stress

Exercise Goals

Sleep   1 2 3 4 5 6 7 8+

Hydration

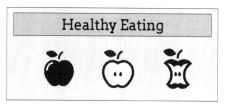
Healthy Eating

My riding goal for the day is: _____

_____

_____

_____

_____

My ride was: _____

_____

_____

_____

_____

_____

_____

_____

Date: _____

Stress

Exercise Goals

Sleep 　1　2　3　4　5　6　7　8+

Hydration

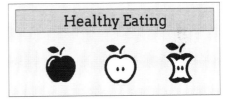
Healthy Eating

My riding goal for the day is:

_____

_____

_____

_____

My ride was: ——————

_____

_____

_____

_____

_____

_____

How will you take extra good care of your body today?

_____

_____

_____

_____

_____

_____

_____

_____

_____

_____

_____

_____

Date: _____

Stress

Exercise Goals

Sleep   1   2   3   4   5   6   7   8+

Hydration

Healthy Eating

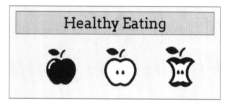

My riding goal for the day is: _____

_____

_____

_____

_____

My ride was: _____

_____

_____

_____

_____

_____

_____

_____

Date: _____

Stress

Sleep   1   2   3   4   5   6   7   8+

Hydration

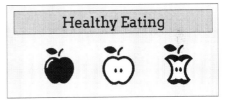

My riding goal for the day is: _____

_____

_____

_____

My ride was: _____

_____

_____

_____

_____

_____

Date: _____

Stress

Exercise Goals

Sleep   1   2   3   4   5   6   7   8+

Hydration

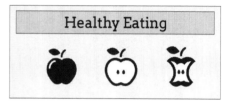

Healthy Eating

My riding goal for the day is: _____

_____

_____

_____

_____

My ride was: _____

_____

_____

_____

_____

_____

_____

_____

Date: _____

Stress

Exercise Goals

Sleep   1   2   3   4   5   6   7   8+

Hydration

Healthy Eating

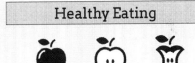

My riding goal for the day is:

_____

_____

_____

_____

My ride was: _____

_____

_____

_____

_____

_____

_____

What did you expect of your ride today? Where did those expectations come from?

_____

_____

_____

_____

_____

_____

_____

_____

_____

Date: _____

Stress

Exercise Goals

Sleep   1   2   3   4   5   6   7   8+

Hydration

Healthy Eating

My riding goal for the day is: _____

_____

_____

_____

_____

My ride was: _____

_____

_____

_____

_____

_____

_____

_____

Date: _____

Stress

Exercise Goals

Sleep   1   2   3   4   5   6   7   8+

Hydration

Healthy Eating

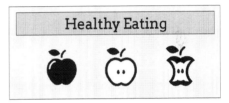

My riding goal for the day is: _____

_____

_____

_____

_____

My ride was: _____

_____

_____

_____

_____

_____

_____

Date: _____

Stress

Exercise Goals

Sleep   1   2   3   4   5   6   7   8+

Hydration

Healthy Eating

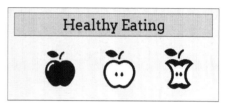

My riding goal for the day is: _____

_____

_____

_____

_____

My ride was: _____

_____

_____

_____

_____

_____

_____

_____

Date: _____

Stress

Exercise Goals

Sleep   1   2   3   4   5   6   7   8+

Hydration

Healthy Eating

My riding goal for the day is:

_____

_____

_____

_____

My ride was: _____

_____

_____

_____

_____

_____

_____

Today, I will create the ride I want by:

_____

_____

_____

_____

_____

_____

_____

_____

_____

_____

_____

Date:_____

Stress

Exercise Goals

Sleep   1   2   3   4   5   6   7   8+

Hydration

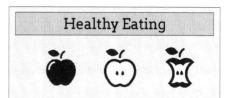
Healthy Eating

My riding goal for the day is: _____

_____

_____

_____

_____

My ride was:_____

_____

_____

_____

_____

_____

_____

_____

Date: _____

Stress

Exercise Goals

Sleep   1   2   3   4   5   6   7   8+

Hydration

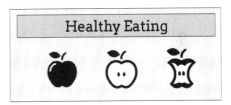

Healthy Eating

My riding goal for the day is: _____

_____

_____

_____

_____

My ride was: _____

_____

_____

_____

_____

_____

_____

_____

Date: _____

Stress

Exercise Goals

Sleep   1   2   3   4   5   6   7   8+

Hydration

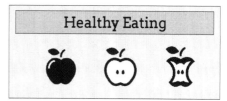

Healthy Eating

My riding goal for the day is: _____

_____

_____

_____

_____

My ride was: _____

_____

_____

_____

_____

_____

_____

_____

Date: _____

Stress

Exercise Goals

Sleep   1 2 3 4 5 6 7 8+

Hydration

Healthy Eating

My riding goal for the day is:

_____

_____

_____

_____

My ride was: _____

_____

_____

_____

_____

_____

_____

This is what makes me believe in my horse:

_____

_____

_____

_____

_____

_____

_____

_____

_____

_____

_____

Date: _____

Stress

Exercise Goals

Sleep   1   2   3   4   5   6   7   8+

Hydration

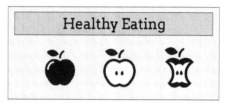
Healthy Eating

My riding goal for the day is: _____

_____

_____

_____

_____

My ride was: _____

_____

_____

_____

_____

_____

_____

_____

Date: _____

Stress

Exercise Goals

Sleep   1   2   3   4   5   6   7   8+

Hydration

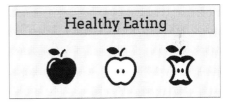

Healthy Eating

My riding goal for the day is: _____

_____

_____

_____

_____

My ride was: _____

_____

_____

_____

_____

_____

_____

Date: _____

Stress

Exercise Goals

Sleep 1　2　3　4　5　6　7　8+

Hydration

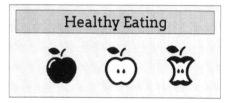
Healthy Eating

My riding goal for the day is: _____

_____

_____

_____

_____

My ride was: _____

_____

_____

_____

_____

_____

_____

_____

Date: _____

Stress

Exercise Goals

Sleep   1   2   3   4   5   6   7   8+

Hydration

Healthy Eating

My riding goal for the day is:

_____

_____

_____

_____

My ride was: ─────────────

_____

_____

_____

_____

_____

_____

I will overcome fear today by:

_____

_____

_____

_____

_____

_____

_____

_____

_____

_____

Date: _____

Stress

Exercise Goals

Sleep   1   2   3   4   5   6   7   8+

Hydration

Healthy Eating

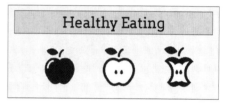

My riding goal for the day is: _____

_____

_____

_____

_____

My ride was: _____

_____

_____

_____

_____

_____

_____

_____

Date: _____

Stress

Exercise Goals

Sleep   1 2 3 4 5 6 7 8+

Hydration

Healthy Eating

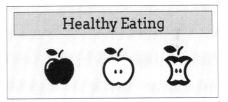

My riding goal for the day is: _____

_____

_____

_____

_____

My ride was: _____

_____

_____

_____

_____

_____

_____

Date: _____

Stress

Exercise Goals

Sleep   1   2   3   4   5   6   7   8+

Hydration

Healthy Eating

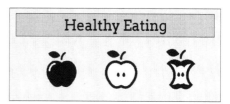

My riding goal for the day is: _____

_____

_____

_____

_____

My ride was: _____

_____

_____

_____

_____

_____

_____

_____

Date: _____

Stress

Exercise Goals

Sleep   1 2 3 4 5 6 7 8+

Hydration

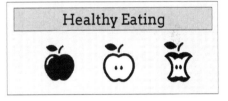
Healthy Eating

My riding goal for the day is:

_____

_____

_____

_____

My ride was: _____

_____

_____

_____

_____

_____

_____

This is my expression of faith in myself.

_____

_____

_____

_____

_____

_____

_____

_____

_____

_____

_____

Date: _____

Stress

Exercise Goals

Sleep 1   2   3   4   5   6   7   8+

Hydration

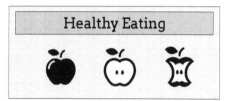

Healthy Eating

My riding goal for the day is: _____

_____

_____

_____

_____

My ride was: _____

_____

_____

_____

_____

_____

_____

_____

_____

Date: _____

Stress

Exercise Goals

Sleep   1   2   3   4   5   6   7   8+

Hydration

Healthy Eating

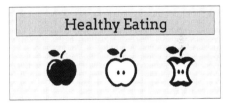

My riding goal for the day is: _____

_____

_____

_____

_____

My ride was: _____

_____

_____

_____

_____

_____

_____

_____

Date: _____

Stress

Exercise Goals

Sleep   1   2   3   4   5   6   7   8+

Hydration

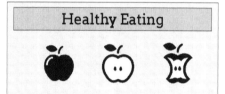

Healthy Eating

My riding goal for the day is: _____

_____

_____

_____

_____

My ride was: _____

_____

_____

_____

_____

_____

_____

_____

Date: _____

Stress

Exercise Goals

Sleep 1　2　3　4　5　6　7　8+

Hydration

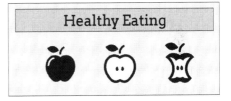
Healthy Eating

My riding goal for the day is:

_____

_____

_____

_____

My ride was: _____

_____

_____

_____

_____

_____

_____

I will show my appreciation for my horse today by:

_____

_____

_____

_____

_____

_____

_____

_____

_____

_____

_____

_____

Date: _____

Stress

Exercise Goals

Sleep   1   2   3   4   5   6   7   8+

Hydration

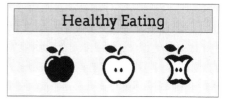
Healthy Eating

My riding goal for the day is: _____

_____

_____

_____

_____

My ride was: _____

_____

_____

_____

_____

_____

_____

_____

Date: _____

Stress

Exercise Goals

Sleep   1   2   3   4   5   6   7   8+

Hydration

Healthy Eating

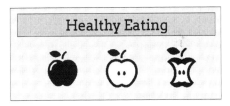

My riding goal for the day is: _____

_____

_____

_____

_____

My ride was: _____

_____

_____

_____

_____

_____

_____

_____

Date: _____

Stress

Sleep   1   2   3   4   5   6   7   8+

Hydration

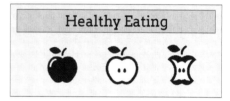

My riding goal for the day is: _____

_____

_____

_____

_____

My ride was: _____

_____

_____

_____

_____

_____

_____

_____

Date: _____

Stress

Exercise Goals

Sleep   1   2   3   4   5   6   7   8+

Hydration

Healthy Eating

My riding goal for the day is:

_____

_____

_____

_____

My ride was: _____

_____

_____

_____

_____

_____

Today, I will celebrate: _____

_____

_____

_____

_____

_____

_____

_____

_____

_____

_____

_____

_____

Date:_____

Stress

Exercise Goals

Sleep 1 2 3 4 5 6 7 8+

Hydration

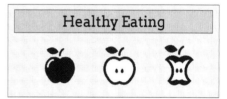

Healthy Eating

My riding goal for the day is: _____

_____

_____

_____

_____

My ride was:_____

_____

_____

_____

_____

_____

_____

Date: _____

Stress

Exercise Goals

Sleep   1 2 3 4 5 6 7 8+

Hydration

Healthy Eating

My riding goal for the day is: _____

_____

_____

_____

_____

My ride was: _____

_____

_____

_____

_____

_____

_____

_____

Date: _____

Stress

Sleep   1   2   3   4   5   6   7   8+

Hydration

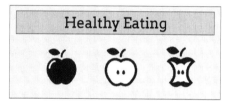

My riding goal for the day is: _____

_____

_____

_____

_____

My ride was: _____

_____

_____

_____

_____

_____

_____

_____

Date: _____

Stress

Exercise Goals

Sleep   1   2   3   4   5   6   7   8+

Hydration

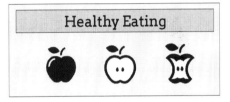
Healthy Eating

My riding goal for the day is:

_____

_____

_____

_____

My ride was: _____

_____

_____

_____

_____

_____

_____

How will you embody kindness today?

_____

_____

_____

_____

_____

_____

_____

_____

_____

_____

_____

Date: _____

Stress

Exercise Goals

Sleep   1   2   3   4   5   6   7   8+

Hydration

Healthy Eating

My riding goal for the day is: _____

_____

_____

_____

_____

My ride was: _____

_____

_____

_____

_____

_____

_____

_____

Date: _____

Stress

Exercise Goals

Sleep   1   2   3   4   5   6   7   8+

Hydration

Healthy Eating

My riding goal for the day is: _____

_____

_____

_____

_____

My ride was: _____

_____

_____

_____

_____

_____

_____

Date: _____

Stress

Exercise Goals

Sleep   1   2   3   4   5   6   7   8+

Hydration

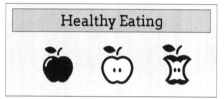
Healthy Eating

My riding goal for the day is: _____

_____

_____

_____

_____

My ride was: _____

_____

_____

_____

_____

_____

_____

_____

Date: _____

Stress

Exercise Goals

Sleep   1   2   3   4   5   6   7   8+

Hydration

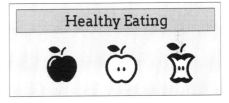

Healthy Eating

My riding goal for the day is:

_____

_____

_____

_____

My ride was: _____

_____

_____

_____

_____

_____

_____

This is what helps me be my best:

_____

_____

_____

_____

_____

_____

_____

_____

_____

_____

_____

_____

_____

Date: _____

Stress

Sleep   1   2   3   4   5   6   7   8+

Hydration

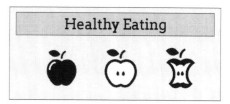

My riding goal for the day is: _____

_____

_____

_____

My ride was: _____

_____

_____

_____

_____

_____

_____

_____

Date: _____

Stress

Exercise Goals

Sleep   1   2   3   4   5   6   7   8+

Hydration

Healthy Eating

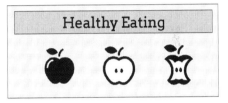

My riding goal for the day is: _____

_____

_____

_____

_____

My ride was: _____

_____

_____

_____

_____

_____

_____

Date: _____

Stress

Exercise Goals

Sleep   1   2   3   4   5   6   7   8+

Hydration

Healthy Eating

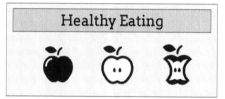

My riding goal for the day is: _____

_____

_____

_____

_____

My ride was: _____

_____

_____

_____

_____

_____

_____

_____

Date: _____

Stress

Sleep 1 2 3 4 5 6 7 8+

Hydration

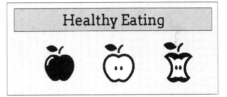

My riding goal for the day is:

_____

_____

_____

_____

My ride was: _____

_____

_____

_____

_____

_____

_____

What is your horse's greatest strength?

_____

_____

_____

_____

_____

_____

_____

_____

_____

_____

_____

Date: _____

Stress

Sleep 1 2 3 4 5 6 7 8+

Hydration

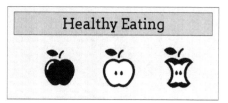

My riding goal for the day is: _____

_____

_____

_____

_____

My ride was: _____

_____

_____

_____

_____

_____

_____

_____

Date: _____

Stress

Exercise Goals

Sleep 1 2 3 4 5 6 7 8+

Hydration

Healthy Eating

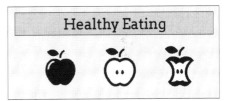

My riding goal for the day is: _____

_____

_____

_____

_____

My ride was: _____

_____

_____

_____

_____

_____

_____

_____

Date: _____

Stress

Exercise Goals

Sleep   1   2   3   4   5   6   7   8+

Hydration

Healthy Eating

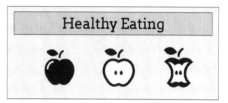

My riding goal for the day is: _____

_____

_____

_____

_____

My ride was: _____

_____

_____

_____

_____

_____

_____

_____

_____

Date: _____

Stress

Exercise Goals

Sleep 1 2 3 4 5 6 7 8+

Hydration

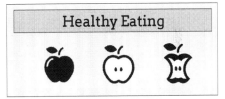

Healthy Eating

My riding goal for the day is: _____

_____

_____

_____

My ride was: _____

_____

_____

_____

_____

_____

Date: _____

Stress

Exercise Goals

Sleep 1 2 3 4 5 6 7 8+

Hydration

Healthy Eating

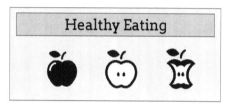

My riding goal for the day is: _____

_____

_____

_____

_____

My ride was: _____

_____

_____

_____

_____

_____

_____

_____

Date: _____

Stress

Exercise Goals

Sleep   1   2   3   4   5   6   7   8+

Hydration

Healthy Eating

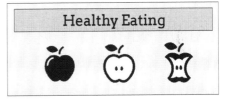

My riding goal for the day is:

_____

_____

_____

_____

My ride was: _____

_____

_____

_____

_____

_____

_____

Concentrate on how it feels to be truly centered in the saddle. How do you find that feeling?

_____

_____

_____

_____

_____

_____

_____

_____

_____

_____

Date: _____

Stress

Sleep   1 2 3 4 5 6 7 8+

Hydration

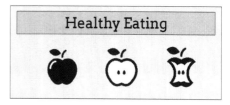

My riding goal for the day is: _____

_____

_____

_____

_____

My ride was: _____

_____

_____

_____

_____

_____

_____

_____

Date: _____

Stress

Exercise Goals

Sleep   1   2   3   4   5   6   7   8+

Hydration

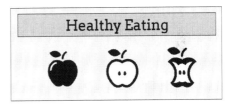

Healthy Eating

My riding goal for the day is: _____

_____

_____

_____

_____

My ride was: _____

_____

_____

_____

_____

_____

_____

Date: _____

Stress

Exercise Goals

Sleep   1   2   3   4   5   6   7   8+

Hydration

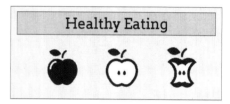
Healthy Eating

My riding goal for the day is: _____

_____

_____

_____

_____

My ride was: _____

_____

_____

_____

_____

_____

_____

_____

Date: _____

Stress

Exercise Goals

Sleep   1   2   3   4   5   6   7   8+

Hydration

Healthy Eating

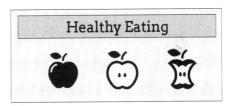

My riding goal for the day is: _____

_____

_____

_____

_____

My ride was: _____

_____

_____

_____

_____

_____

_____

_____

Date: _____

Stress

Exercise Goals

Sleep 1   2   3   4   5   6   7   8+

Hydration

Healthy Eating

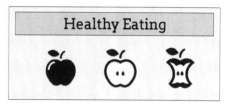

My riding goal for the day is: _____

_____

_____

_____

_____

My ride was: _____

_____

_____

_____

_____

_____

_____

_____

Date: _____

Stress

Exercise Goals

Sleep   1   2   3   4   5   6   7   8+

Hydration

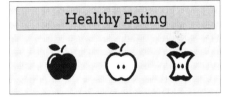

Healthy Eating

My riding goal for the day is:

_____

_____

_____

_____

My ride was: _____

_____

_____

_____

_____

_____

_____

This is what helps my horse be her/his best:

_____

_____

_____

_____

_____

_____

_____

_____

_____

_____

Date: _____

Stress

Exercise Goals

Sleep   1   2   3   4   5   6   7   8+

Hydration

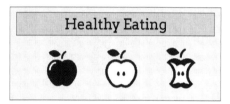

Healthy Eating

My riding goal for the day is: _____

_____

_____

_____

_____

My ride was: _____

_____

_____

_____

_____

_____

_____

_____

Date: _____

Stress

Exercise Goals

Sleep 1 2 3 4 5 6 7 8+

Hydration

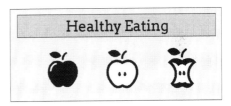

Healthy Eating

My riding goal for the day is: _____

_____

_____

_____

_____

My ride was: _____

_____

_____

_____

_____

_____

_____

Date: _____

Stress

Exercise Goals

Sleep   1   2   3   4   5   6   7   8+

Hydration

Healthy Eating

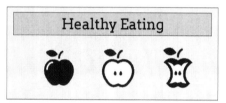

My riding goal for the day is: _____

_____

_____

_____

_____

My ride was: _____

_____

_____

_____

_____

_____

_____

_____

Date: _____

Stress

Exercise Goals

Sleep   1   2   3   4   5   6   7   8+

Hydration

Healthy Eating

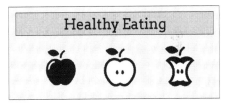

My riding goal for the day is: _____

_____

_____

_____

_____

My ride was: _____

_____

_____

_____

_____

_____

_____

_____

Date:_____

Stress

Exercise Goals

Sleep   1   2   3   4   5   6   7   8+

Hydration

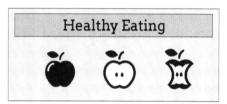

Healthy Eating

My riding goal for the day is: _____

_____

_____

_____

_____

My ride was:_____

_____

_____

_____

_____

_____

_____

_____

Date: _____

Stress

Sleep   1   2   3   4   5   6   7   8+

Hydration

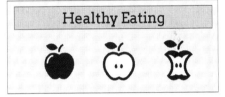

My riding goal for the day is:

_____

_____

_____

_____

My ride was: _____

_____

_____

_____

_____

_____

_____

Today I am grateful for:_____

_____

_____

_____

_____

_____

_____

_____

_____

_____

_____

_____

_____

Date: _____

Stress

Exercise Goals

Sleep   1   2   3   4   5   6   7   8+

Hydration

Healthy Eating

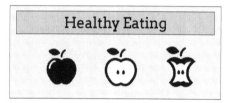

My riding goal for the day is: _____

_____

_____

_____

_____

My ride was: _____

_____

_____

_____

_____

_____

_____

_____

Date: _____

Stress

Exercise Goals

Sleep   1 2 3 4 5 6 7 8+

Hydration

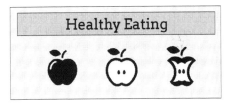

Healthy Eating

My riding goal for the day is: _____

_____

_____

_____

_____

My ride was: _____

_____

_____

_____

_____

_____

_____

_____

Date:_____

Stress

Exercise Goals

Sleep   1   2   3   4   5   6   7   8+

Hydration

Healthy Eating

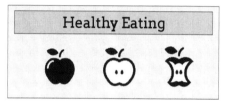

My riding goal for the day is: _____

_____

_____

_____

_____

My ride was: _____

_____

_____

_____

_____

_____

_____

_____

Date: _____

Stress

Exercise Goals

Sleep   1   2   3   4   5   6   7   8+

Hydration

Healthy Eating

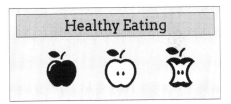

My riding goal for the day is: _____

_____

_____

_____

_____

My ride was: _____

_____

_____

_____

_____

_____

_____

_____

Date: _____

Stress

Exercise Goals

Sleep   1   2   3   4   5   6   7   8+

Hydration

Healthy Eating

My riding goal for the day is: _____

_____

_____

_____

_____

My ride was: _____

_____

_____

_____

_____

_____

_____

_____

Date: _____

Stress

Exercise Goals

Sleep   1   2   3   4   5   6   7   8+

Hydration

Healthy Eating

My riding goal for the day is:

_____
_____
_____
_____

My ride was: _____

_____
_____
_____
_____
_____
_____

I feel most free when I: _____

_____
_____
_____
_____
_____
_____
_____
_____
_____
_____
_____
_____
_____
_____

Date: _____

Stress

Exercise Goals

Sleep   1   2   3   4   5   6   7   8+

Hydration

Healthy Eating

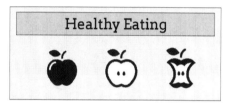

My riding goal for the day is: _____

_____

_____

_____

_____

My ride was: _____

_____

_____

_____

_____

_____

_____

_____

Date: _____

Stress

Exercise Goals

Sleep 　　1　2　3　4　5　6　7　8+

Hydration

Healthy Eating

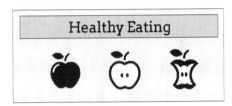

My riding goal for the day is: _____

_____

_____

_____

_____

My ride was: _____

_____

_____

_____

_____

_____

_____

_____

Date:_____

Stress

Exercise Goals

Sleep 1   2   3   4   5   6   7   8+

Hydration

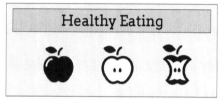
Healthy Eating

My riding goal for the day is: _____

_____

_____

_____

_____

My ride was:_____

_____

_____

_____

_____

_____

_____

_____

Date: _____

Stress

Exercise Goals

Sleep   1   2   3   4   5   6   7   8+

Hydration

Healthy Eating

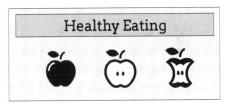

My riding goal for the day is: _____

_____

_____

_____

_____

My ride was: _____

_____

_____

_____

_____

_____

_____

Date: _____

Stress

Sleep   1   2   3   4   5   6   7   8+

Hydration

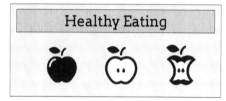

My riding goal for the day is: _____

_____

_____

_____

_____

My ride was: _____

_____

_____

_____

_____

_____

_____

_____

_____

Date: _____

Stress

Exercise Goals

Sleep 1 2 3 4 5 6 7 8+

Hydration

Healthy Eating

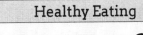

My riding goal for the day is:

_____

_____

_____

_____

My ride was: _____

_____

_____

_____

_____

_____

_____

How will you connect your mind and your body as you ride?

_____

_____

_____

_____

_____

_____

_____

_____

_____

Date: _____

Stress

Sleep   1   2   3   4   5   6   7   8+

Hydration

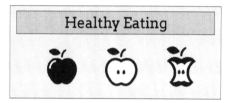

My riding goal for the day is: _____

_____

_____

_____

_____

My ride was: _____

_____

_____

_____

_____

_____

_____

_____

_____

Date: _____

Stress

Exercise Goals

Sleep   1   2   3   4   5   6   7   8+

Hydration

Healthy Eating

My riding goal for the day is: _____

_____

_____

_____

_____

My ride was: _____

_____

_____

_____

_____

_____

_____

_____

Date: _____

Stress

Exercise Goals

Sleep   1   2   3   4   5   6   7   8+

Hydration

Healthy Eating

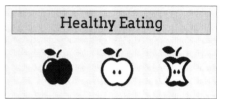

My riding goal for the day is: _____

_____

_____

_____

_____

My ride was: _____

_____

_____

_____

_____

_____

_____

_____

_____

Date: _____

Stress

Exercise Goals

Sleep 1 2 3 4 5 6 7 8+

Hydration

Healthy Eating

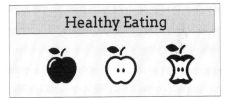

My riding goal for the day is: _____

_____

_____

_____

_____

My ride was: _____

_____

_____

_____

_____

_____

_____

Date: _____

Stress

Exercise Goals

Sleep 　　1　2　3　4　5　6　7　8+

Hydration

Healthy Eating

My riding goal for the day is: _____

_____

_____

_____

_____

My ride was: _____

_____

_____

_____

_____

_____

_____

_____

Date: _____

Stress

Exercise Goals

Sleep   1 2 3 4 5 6 7 8+

Hydration

Healthy Eating

My riding goal for the day is:

_____

_____

_____

_____

My ride was: _____

_____

_____

_____

_____

_____

What helps you to focus when you're riding?

_____

_____

_____

_____

_____

_____

_____

_____

_____

_____

_____

Date: _____

Stress

Exercise Goals

Sleep   1   2   3   4   5   6   7   8+

Hydration

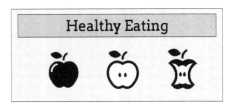

Healthy Eating

My riding goal for the day is: _____

_____

_____

_____

_____

My ride was: _____

_____

_____

_____

_____

_____

_____

Date: _____

Stress

Exercise Goals

Sleep   1   2   3   4   5   6   7   8+

Hydration

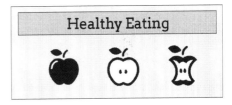

Healthy Eating

My riding goal for the day is: _____

_____

_____

_____

_____

My ride was: _____

_____

_____

_____

_____

_____

_____

Date: _____

Stress

Sleep   1   2   3   4   5   6   7   8+

Hydration

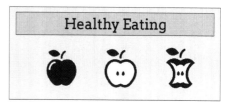

My riding goal for the day is: _____

_____

_____

_____

_____

My ride was: _____

_____

_____

_____

_____

_____

_____

Date: _____

Stress

Exercise Goals

Sleep   1   2   3   4   5   6   7   8+

Hydration

Healthy Eating

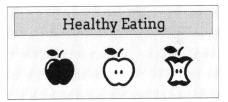

My riding goal for the day is: _____

_____

_____

_____

_____

My ride was: _____

_____

_____

_____

_____

_____

_____

Date: _____

Stress

Sleep   1   2   3   4   5   6   7   8+

Hydration

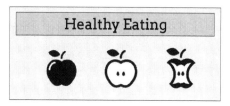

My riding goal for the day is: _____

_____

_____

_____

My ride was: _____

_____

_____

_____

_____

_____

_____

_____

Date: _____

Stress

Exercise Goals

Sleep 1 2 3 4 5 6 7 8+

Hydration

Healthy Eating

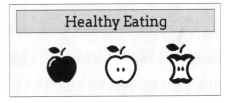

My riding goal for the day is:

_____

_____

_____

_____

My ride was: _____

_____

_____

_____

_____

_____

_____

I admire the way my horse and I:

_____

_____

_____

_____

_____

_____

_____

_____

_____

_____

_____

_____

Date: _____

Stress

Sleep   1   2   3   4   5   6   7   8+

Hydration

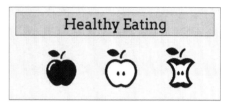

My riding goal for the day is: _____

_____

_____

_____

_____

My ride was: _____

_____

_____

_____

_____

_____

_____

_____

Date: _____

Stress

Sleep   1   2   3   4   5   6   7   8+

Hydration

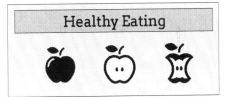

My riding goal for the day is: _____

_____

_____

_____

_____

My ride was: _____

_____

_____

_____

_____

_____

_____

Date: _____

Stress

Exercise Goals

Sleep   1   2   3   4   5   6   7   8+

Hydration

Healthy Eating

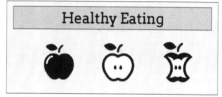

My riding goal for the day is: _____

_____

_____

_____

_____

My ride was: _____

_____

_____

_____

_____

_____

_____

Date: _____

Stress

Exercise Goals

Sleep   1 2 3 4 5 6 7 8+

Hydration

Healthy Eating

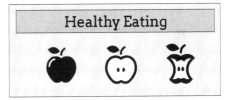

My riding goal for the day is: _____
_____
_____
_____
_____

My ride was: _____
_____
_____
_____
_____
_____
_____
_____

Date:_____

Stress

Exercise Goals

Sleep   1 2 3 4 5 6 7 8+

Hydration

Healthy Eating

My riding goal for the day is: _____

_____

_____

_____

_____

My ride was:_____

_____

_____

_____

_____

_____

_____

_____

Date: _____

Stress

Exercise Goals

Sleep   1   2   3   4   5   6   7   8+

Hydration

Healthy Eating

My riding goal for the day is:

_____

_____

_____

_____

My ride was: _____

_____

_____

_____

_____

_____

_____

Who helps you to ride your very best? How can you say thank-you?

_____

_____

_____

_____

_____

_____

_____

_____

_____

_____

Date: _____

Stress

Sleep 1 2 3 4 5 6 7 8+

Hydration

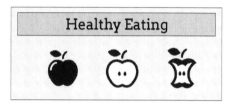

My riding goal for the day is: _____

_____

_____

_____

_____

My ride was: _____

_____

_____

_____

_____

_____

_____

_____

_____

Date: _____

Stress

Exercise Goals

Sleep   1   2   3   4   5   6   7   8+

Hydration

Healthy Eating

My riding goal for the day is: _____

_____

_____

_____

_____

My ride was: _____

_____

_____

_____

_____

_____

_____

Date: _____

Stress

Exercise Goals

Sleep   1   2   3   4   5   6   7   8+

Hydration

Healthy Eating
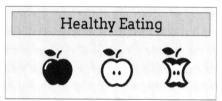

My riding goal for the day is: _____

_____

_____

_____

_____

My ride was: _____

_____

_____

_____

_____

_____

_____

Date: _____

Stress

Exercise Goals

Sleep   1   2   3   4   5   6   7   8+

Hydration

Healthy Eating

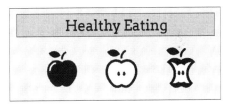

My riding goal for the day is: _____

_____

_____

_____

_____

My ride was: _____

_____

_____

_____

_____

_____

_____

_____

Date:_____

Stress

Exercise Goals

Sleep   1   2   3   4   5   6   7   8+

Hydration

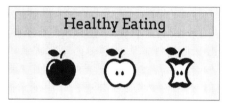

Healthy Eating

My riding goal for the day is: _____

_____

_____

_____

_____

My ride was: _____

_____

_____

_____

_____

_____

_____

_____

Date: _____

Stress

Exercise Goals

Sleep   1   2   3   4   5   6   7   8+

Hydration

Healthy Eating

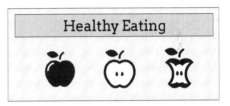

My riding goal for the day is:

_____

_____

_____

_____

My ride was: _____

_____

_____

_____

_____

_____

_____

_____

My horse enjoys herself /
himself most when we:

Date: _____

Stress

Exercise Goals

Sleep 1 2 3 4 5 6 7 8+

Hydration

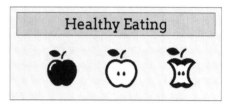
Healthy Eating

My riding goal for the day is: _____
_____
_____
_____
_____

My ride was: _____
_____
_____
_____
_____
_____
_____
_____

Date: _____

Stress

Exercise Goals

Sleep 1   2   3   4   5   6   7   8+

Hydration

Healthy Eating

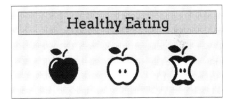

My riding goal for the day is: _____

_____

_____

_____

_____

My ride was: _____

_____

_____

_____

_____

_____

_____

_____

Date: _____

Stress

Sleep   1   2   3   4   5   6   7   8+

Hydration

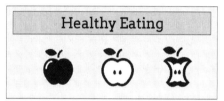

My riding goal for the day is: _____

_____

_____

_____

_____

My ride was: _____

_____

_____

_____

_____

_____

_____

_____

_____

Date: _____

Stress

Exercise Goals

Sleep   1   2   3   4   5   6   7   8+

Hydration

Healthy Eating

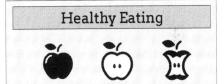

My riding goal for the day is: _____

_____

_____

_____

_____

My ride was: _____

_____

_____

_____

_____

_____

_____

_____

Date: _____

Stress

Exercise Goals

Sleep   1   2   3   4   5   6   7   8+

Hydration

Healthy Eating

My riding goal for the day is: _____

_____

_____

_____

_____

My ride was: _____

_____

_____

_____

_____

_____

_____

_____

Date: _____

Stress

Exercise Goals

Sleep   1 2 3 4 5 6 7 8+

Hydration

Healthy Eating

My riding goal for the day is:

_____

_____

_____

_____

My ride was: _____

_____

_____

_____

_____

_____

_____

For me, balance is: _____

_____

_____

_____

_____

_____

_____

_____

_____

_____

_____

_____

Date: _____

Stress

Exercise Goals

Sleep   1   2   3   4   5   6   7   8+

Hydration

Healthy Eating

My riding goal for the day is: _____

_____

_____

_____

_____

My ride was: _____

_____

_____

_____

_____

_____

_____

Date: _____

Stress

Exercise Goals

Sleep   1   2   3   4   5   6   7   8+

Hydration

Healthy Eating

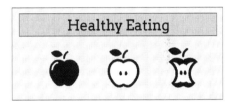

My riding goal for the day is: _____

_____

_____

_____

_____

My ride was: _____

_____

_____

_____

_____

_____

_____

_____

Date: _____

Stress

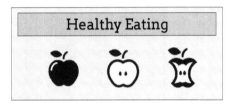
Exercise Goals

Sleep   1   2   3   4   5   6   7   8+

Hydration

Healthy Eating

My riding goal for the day is: _____

_____

_____

_____

_____

My ride was: _____

_____

_____

_____

_____

_____

_____

Date: _____

Stress

Exercise Goals

Sleep   1   2   3   4   5   6   7   8+

Hydration

Healthy Eating

My riding goal for the day is: _____

_____

_____

_____

_____

My ride was: _____

_____

_____

_____

_____

_____

_____

Date:_____

Stress

Exercise Goals

Sleep   1   2   3   4   5   6   7   8+

Hydration

Healthy Eating

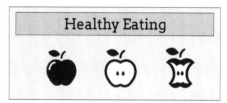

My riding goal for the day is: _____

_____

_____

_____

_____

My ride was:_____

_____

_____

_____

_____

_____

_____

Date: _____

Stress

Exercise Goals

Sleep 1 2 3 4 5 6 7 8+

Hydration

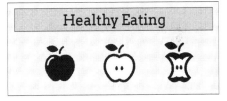

Healthy Eating

My riding goal for the day is:

_____

_____

_____

_____

My ride was: _____

_____

_____

_____

_____

_____

_____

How will you nurture your
and your horse's emotional
well-being during your ride
today?

_____

_____

_____

_____

_____

_____

_____

_____

_____

_____

Date: _____

Stress

Exercise Goals

Sleep   1   2   3   4   5   6   7   8+

Hydration

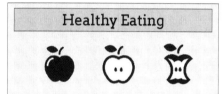

Healthy Eating

My riding goal for the day is: _____

_____

_____

_____

_____

My ride was: _____

_____

_____

_____

_____

_____

_____

_____

Date: _____

Stress

Sleep   1   2   3   4   5   6   7   8+

Hydration

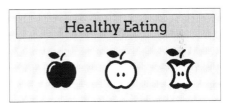

My riding goal for the day is: _____

_____

_____

_____

_____

My ride was: _____

_____

_____

_____

_____

_____

_____

Date: _____

Stress

Exercise Goals

Sleep   1   2   3   4   5   6   7   8+

Hydration

Healthy Eating

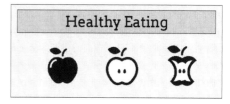

My riding goal for the day is: _____

_____

_____

_____

_____

My ride was: _____

_____

_____

_____

_____

_____

_____

_____

Date: _____

Stress

Exercise Goals

Sleep 1 2 3 4 5 6 7 8+

Hydration

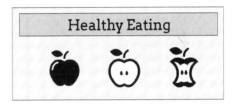
Healthy Eating

My riding goal for the day is: _____

_____

_____

_____

_____

My ride was: _____

_____

_____

_____

_____

_____

_____

_____

Date: _____

Stress

Exercise Goals

Sleep   1   2   3   4   5   6   7   8+

Hydration

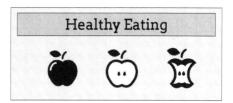

Healthy Eating

My riding goal for the day is: _____

_____

_____

_____

_____

My ride was: _____

_____

_____

_____

_____

_____

_____

_____

Date: _____

Stress

Sleep 1   2   3   4   5   6   7   8+

Hydration

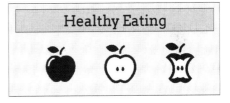

My riding goal for the day is:

_____

_____

_____

_____

My ride was: _____

_____

_____

_____

_____

_____

_____

I will practice good self-care in the saddle by:

_____

_____

_____

_____

_____

_____

_____

_____

_____

_____

_____

_____

Date: _____

Stress

Exercise Goals

Sleep   1   2   3   4   5   6   7   8+

Hydration

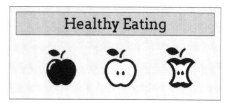

Healthy Eating

My riding goal for the day is: _____

_____

_____

_____

_____

My ride was: _____

_____

_____

_____

_____

_____

_____

_____

Date: _____

Stress

Exercise Goals

Sleep 1 2 3 4 5 6 7 8+

Hydration

Healthy Eating

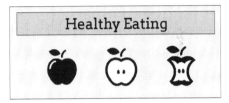

My riding goal for the day is: _____

_____

_____

_____

My ride was: _____

_____

_____

_____

_____

Date: _____

Stress

Exercise Goals

Sleep   1   2   3   4   5   6   7   8+

Hydration

Healthy Eating

My riding goal for the day is: _____

_____

_____

_____

_____

My ride was: _____

_____

_____

_____

_____

_____

_____

_____

Date: _____

Stress

Sleep   1   2   3   4   5   6   7   8+

Hydration

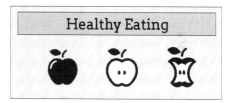

My riding goal for the day is: _____

_____

_____

_____

_____

My ride was: _____

_____

_____

_____

_____

_____

_____

_____

_____

Date: _____

Stress

Exercise Goals

Sleep   1   2   3   4   5   6   7   8+

Hydration

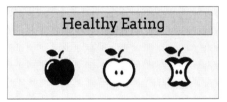

Healthy Eating

My riding goal for the day is: _____

_____

_____

_____

My ride was: _____

_____

_____

_____

_____

_____

Date: _____

Stress

Exercise Goals

Sleep   1 2 3 4 5 6 7 8+

Hydration

Healthy Eating

My riding goal for the day is:

_____

_____

_____

_____

My ride was: ——————————

_____

_____

_____

_____

_____

_____

_____

What is your attitude towards your riding today? How is it impacting your riding?

_____

_____

_____

_____

_____

_____

_____

_____

_____

_____

Date: _____

Stress

Exercise Goals

Sleep   1   2   3   4   5   6   7   8+

Hydration

Healthy Eating

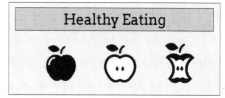

My riding goal for the day is: _____

_____

_____

_____

_____

My ride was: _____

_____

_____

_____

_____

_____

_____

_____

Date: _____

Stress

Exercise Goals

Sleep   1   2   3   4   5   6   7   8+

Hydration

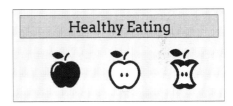
Healthy Eating

My riding goal for the day is: _____

_____

_____

_____

_____

My ride was: _____

_____

_____

_____

_____

_____

_____

_____

Date: _____

Stress

Exercise Goals

Sleep   1   2   3   4   5   6   7   8+

Hydration

Healthy Eating

My riding goal for the day is: _____

_____

_____

_____

_____

My ride was: _____

_____

_____

_____

_____

_____

_____

_____

Date: _____

Stress

Exercise Goals

Sleep   1 2 3 4 5 6 7 8+

Hydration

Healthy Eating

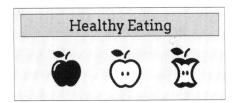

My riding goal for the day is: _____

_____

_____

_____

_____

My ride was: _____

_____

_____

_____

_____

_____

_____

_____

Date:_____

Stress

Sleep   1   2   3   4   5   6   7   8+

Hydration

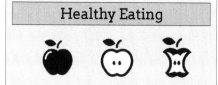

My riding goal for the day is: _____

_____

_____

_____

_____

My ride was: _____

_____

_____

_____

_____

_____

_____

_____

_____

Date: _____

Stress

Exercise Goals

Sleep   1   2   3   4   5   6   7   8+

Hydration

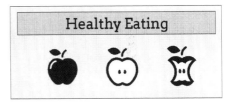
Healthy Eating

My riding goal for the day is:

_____

_____

_____

_____

My ride was: _____

_____

_____

_____

_____

_____

_____

I am strongest when I: _____

_____

_____

_____

_____

_____

_____

_____

_____

_____

_____

_____

Date: _____

Stress

Exercise Goals

Sleep   1   2   3   4   5   6   7   8+

Hydration

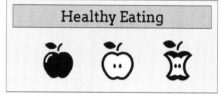
Healthy Eating

My riding goal for the day is: _____

_____

_____

_____

_____

My ride was: _____

_____

_____

_____

_____

_____

_____

_____

_____

Date: _____

Stress

Exercise Goals

Sleep   1   2   3   4   5   6   7   8+

Hydration

Healthy Eating

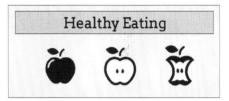

My riding goal for the day is: _____

_____

_____

_____

_____

My ride was: _____

_____

_____

_____

_____

_____

_____

Date: _____

Stress

Exercise Goals

Sleep   1 2 3 4 5 6 7 8+

Hydration

Healthy Eating

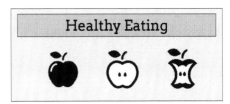

My riding goal for the day is: _____

_____

_____

_____

_____

My ride was: _____

_____

_____

_____

_____

_____

_____

Date: _____

Stress

Exercise Goals

Sleep   1   2   3   4   5   6   7   8+

Hydration

Healthy Eating

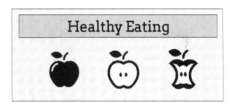

My riding goal for the day is: _____

_____

_____

_____

_____

My ride was: _____

_____

_____

_____

_____

_____

_____

Stress

Exercise Goals

Sleep   1   2   3   4   5   6   7   8+

Hydration

Healthy Eating

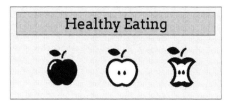

My riding goal for the day is: _____

_____

_____

_____

_____

My ride was: _____

_____

_____

_____

_____

_____

_____

Date: _____

Stress

Exercise Goals

Sleep   1   2   3   4   5   6   7   8+

Hydration

Healthy Eating

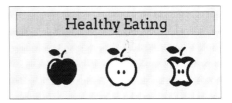

My riding goal for the day is:

_____

_____

_____

_____

My ride was: _____

_____

_____

_____

_____

_____

_____

_____

This is how my horse helps me to be a better person:

_____

_____

_____

_____

_____

_____

_____

_____

_____

_____

_____

_____

_____

Date: _____

Stress

Exercise Goals

Sleep   1   2   3   4   5   6   7   8+

Hydration

Healthy Eating

My riding goal for the day is: _____

_____

_____

_____

_____

My ride was: _____

_____

_____

_____

_____

_____

_____

_____

Date: _____

Stress

Exercise Goals

Sleep   1   2   3   4   5   6   7   8+

Hydration

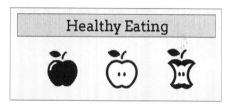

Healthy Eating

My riding goal for the day is: _____

_____

_____

_____

_____

My ride was: _____

_____

_____

_____

_____

_____

_____

_____

Date:_____

Stress

Exercise Goals

Sleep   1   2   3   4   5   6   7   8+

Hydration

Healthy Eating

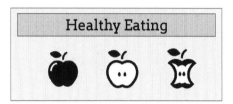

My riding goal for the day is: _____

_____

_____

_____

_____

My ride was:_____

_____

_____

_____

_____

_____

_____

Date: _____

Stress

Exercise Goals

Sleep   1   2   3   4   5   6   7   8+

Hydration

Healthy Eating

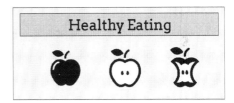

My riding goal for the day is: _____

_____

_____

_____

_____

My ride was: _____

_____

_____

_____

_____

_____

_____

_____

Date: _____

Stress

Exercise Goals

Sleep   1   2   3   4   5   6   7   8+

Hydration

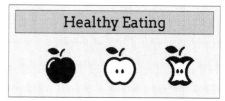

Healthy Eating

My riding goal for the day is: _____

_____

_____

_____

_____

My ride was: _____

_____

_____

_____

_____

_____

_____

_____

_____

Date: _____

Stress

Exercise Goals

Sleep   1   2   3   4   5   6   7   8+

Hydration

Healthy Eating

My riding goal for the day is:

_____

_____

_____

_____

My ride was: ——————————

_____

_____

_____

_____

_____

This is how I help my horse be a better horse:

_____

_____

_____

_____

_____

_____

_____

_____

_____

_____

_____

Date: _____

Stress

Exercise Goals

Sleep 1　2　3　4　5　6　7　8+

Hydration

Healthy Eating

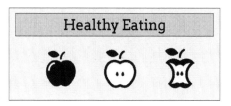

My riding goal for the day is: _____

_____

_____

_____

_____

My ride was: _____

_____

_____

_____

_____

_____

_____

Date: _____

Stress

Exercise Goals

Sleep   1   2   3   4   5   6   7   8+

Hydration

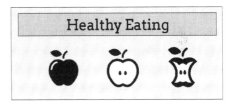

Healthy Eating

My riding goal for the day is: _____

_____

_____

_____

_____

My ride was: _____

_____

_____

_____

_____

_____

_____

_____

_____

Date: _____

Stress

Exercise Goals

Sleep   1   2   3   4   5   6   7   8+

Hydration

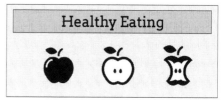
Healthy Eating

My riding goal for the day is: _____

_____

_____

_____

_____

My ride was: _____

_____

_____

_____

_____

_____

_____

_____

Date: _____

Stress

Exercise Goals

Sleep   1   2   3   4   5   6   7   8+

Hydration

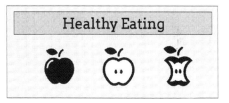
Healthy Eating

My riding goal for the day is: _____

_____

_____

_____

_____

My ride was: _____

_____

_____

_____

_____

_____

_____

_____

Date: _____

Stress

Exercise Goals

Sleep 1 2 3 4 5 6 7 8+

Hydration

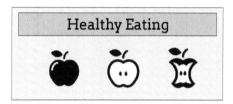

Healthy Eating

My riding goal for the day is: _____

_____

_____

_____

_____

My ride was: _____

_____

_____

_____

_____

_____

_____

Date: _____

Stress

Exercise Goals

Sleep   1   2   3   4   5   6   7   8+

Hydration

Healthy Eating

My riding goal for the day is:

_____

_____

_____

_____

My ride was: _____

_____

_____

_____

_____

_____

_____

What role does riding play in keeping you balanced in your life?

_____

_____

_____

_____

_____

_____

_____

_____

_____

_____

Date: _____

Stress

Exercise Goals

Sleep   1   2   3   4   5   6   7   8+

Hydration

Healthy Eating

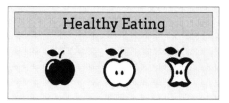

My riding goal for the day is: _____

_____

_____

_____

_____

My ride was: _____

_____

_____

_____

_____

_____

_____

Date: _____

Stress

Exercise Goals

Sleep 1 2 3 4 5 6 7 8+

Hydration

Healthy Eating

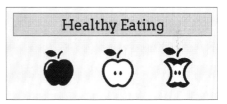

My riding goal for the day is: _____

_____

_____

_____

_____

My ride was: _____

_____

_____

_____

_____

_____

_____

Date: _____

Stress

Exercise Goals

Sleep   1   2   3   4   5   6   7   8+

Hydration

Healthy Eating

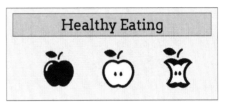

My riding goal for the day is: _____

_____

_____

_____

_____

My ride was: _____

_____

_____

_____

_____

_____

_____

Date: _____

Stress

Exercise Goals

Sleep 1 2 3 4 5 6 7 8+

Hydration

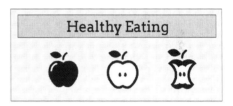
Healthy Eating

My riding goal for the day is: _____

_____

_____

_____

_____

My ride was: _____

_____

_____

_____

_____

_____

_____

_____

Date: _____

Stress

Sleep   1   2   3   4   5   6   7   8+

Hydration

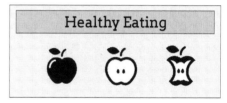

My riding goal for the day is: _____

_____

_____

_____

_____

My ride was: _____

_____

_____

_____

_____

_____

_____

_____

Date: _____

Stress

Exercise Goals

Sleep   1   2   3   4   5   6   7   8+

Hydration

Healthy Eating

My riding goal for the day is:

_____

_____

_____

_____

My ride was: _____

_____

_____

_____

_____

_____

_____

What do you most need to stop thinking about so you can concentrate on your ride? How will you put those thoughts away?

_____

_____

_____

_____

_____

_____

_____

_____

_____

_____

Date: _____

Stress

Exercise Goals

Sleep   1   2   3   4   5   6   7   8+

Hydration

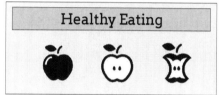

Healthy Eating

My riding goal for the day is: _____

_____

_____

_____

_____

My ride was: _____

_____

_____

_____

_____

_____

_____

_____

_____

Date: _____

Stress

Exercise Goals

Sleep 1   2   3   4   5   6   7   8+

Hydration

Healthy Eating

My riding goal for the day is: _____

_____

_____

_____

_____

My ride was: _____

_____

_____

_____

_____

_____

_____

_____

Date: _____

Stress

Exercise Goals

Sleep   1   2   3   4   5   6   7   8+

Hydration

Healthy Eating

My riding goal for the day is: _____

_____

_____

_____

_____

My ride was: _____

_____

_____

_____

_____

_____

_____

_____

Date: _____

Stress

Exercise Goals

Sleep 1 2 3 4 5 6 7 8+

Hydration

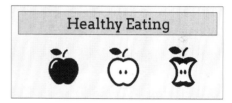
Healthy Eating

My riding goal for the day is: _____

_____

_____

_____

_____

My ride was: _____

_____

_____

_____

_____

_____

_____

_____

_____

Date: _____

Stress

Exercise Goals

Sleep   1   2   3   4   5   6   7   8+

Hydration

Healthy Eating

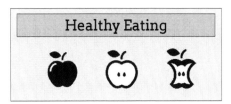

My riding goal for the day is: _____

_____

_____

_____

_____

My ride was: _____

_____

_____

_____

_____

_____

_____

_____

Date: _____

Stress

Exercise Goals

Sleep 1   2   3   4   5   6   7   8+

Hydration

Healthy Eating

My riding goal for the day is:

_____

_____

_____

_____

My ride was: _____

_____

_____

_____

_____

_____

_____

This is how I plan to share a connection with my horse today:

_____

_____

_____

_____

_____

_____

_____

_____

_____

_____

Date: _____

Stress

Exercise Goals

Sleep   1   2   3   4   5   6   7   8+

Hydration

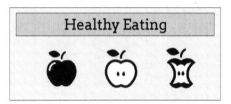
Healthy Eating

My riding goal for the day is: _____

_____

_____

_____

_____

My ride was: _____

_____

_____

_____

_____

_____

_____

Date: _____

Stress

Exercise Goals

Sleep   1   2   3   4   5   6   7   8+

Hydration

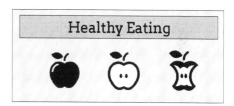

Healthy Eating

My riding goal for the day is: _____

_____

_____

_____

_____

My ride was: _____

_____

_____

_____

_____

_____

_____

_____

_____

Date: _____

Stress

Exercise Goals

Sleep   1   2   3   4   5   6   7   8+

Hydration

Healthy Eating

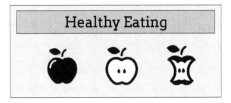

My riding goal for the day is: _____

_____

_____

_____

_____

My ride was: _____

_____

_____

_____

_____

_____

_____

Date: _____

Stress

Exercise Goals

Sleep   1   2   3   4   5   6   7   8+

Hydration

Healthy Eating

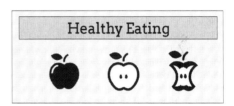

My riding goal for the day is: _____

_____

_____

_____

_____

My ride was: _____

_____

_____

_____

_____

_____

_____

Date: _____

Stress

Exercise Goals

Sleep   1   2   3   4   5   6   7   8+

Hydration

Healthy Eating

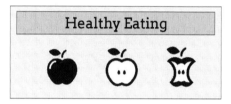

My riding goal for the day is: _____

_____

_____

_____

_____

My ride was: _____

_____

_____

_____

_____

_____

_____

Date: _____

Stress

Exercise Goals

Sleep   1 2 3 4 5 6 7 8+

Hydration

Healthy Eating

My riding goal for the day is:

_____

_____

_____

_____

My ride was: _____

_____

_____

_____

_____

_____

This is what I need to give my best today:

_____

_____

_____

_____

_____

_____

_____

_____

_____

_____

_____

Date: _____

Stress

Exercise Goals

Sleep   1   2   3   4   5   6   7   8+

Hydration

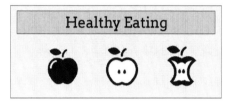
Healthy Eating

My riding goal for the day is: _____
_____
_____
_____
_____

My ride was: _____
_____
_____
_____
_____
_____
_____

Date: _____

Stress

Exercise Goals

Sleep 1 2 3 4 5 6 7 8+

Hydration

Healthy Eating

My riding goal for the day is: _____

_____

_____

_____

_____

My ride was: _____

_____

_____

_____

_____

_____

_____

_____

Date: _____

Exercise Goals

Sleep   1   2   3   4   5   6   7   8+

Hydration

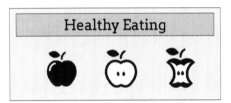
Healthy Eating

My riding goal for the day is: _____

_____

_____

_____

_____

My ride was: _____

_____

_____

_____

_____

_____

_____

Date: _____

Stress

Exercise Goals

Sleep   1   2   3   4   5   6   7   8+

Hydration

Healthy Eating

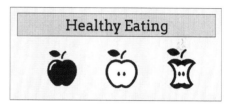

My riding goal for the day is: _____

_____

_____

_____

_____

My ride was: _____

_____

_____

_____

_____

_____

_____

_____

Date: _____

Stress

Exercise Goals

Sleep   1   2   3   4   5   6   7   8+

Hydration

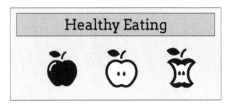
Healthy Eating

My riding goal for the day is: _____

_____

_____

_____

_____

My ride was: _____

_____

_____

_____

_____

_____

_____

_____

Date: _____

Stress

Exercise Goals

Sleep  1   2   3   4   5   6   7   8+

Hydration

Healthy Eating

My riding goal for the day is:

_____

_____

_____

_____

My ride was: _____

_____

_____

_____

_____

_____

_____

How will you find peace in the saddle today?

_____

_____

_____

_____

_____

_____

_____

_____

_____

_____

_____

_____

Date: _____

Stress

Sleep   1   2   3   4   5   6   7   8+

Hydration

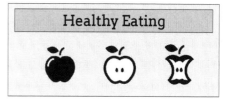

My riding goal for the day is: _____

_____

_____

_____

_____

My ride was: _____

_____

_____

_____

_____

_____

_____

_____

Date: _____

Stress

Sleep   1 2 3 4 5 6 7 8+

Hydration

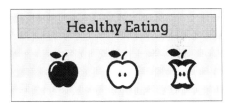

My riding goal for the day is: _____

_____

_____

_____

_____

My ride was: _____

_____

_____

_____

_____

_____

_____

_____

Date:_____

Stress

Exercise Goals

Sleep   1   2   3   4   5   6   7   8+

Hydration

Healthy Eating

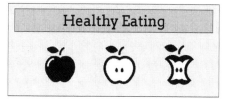

My riding goal for the day is: _____

_____

_____

_____

_____

My ride was: _____

_____

_____

_____

_____

_____

_____

_____

Date: _____

Stress

Exercise Goals

Sleep 1   2   3   4   5   6   7   8+

Hydration

Healthy Eating

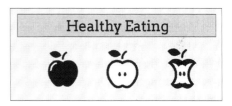

My riding goal for the day is: _____

_____

_____

_____

_____

My ride was: _____

_____

_____

_____

_____

_____

_____

_____

Date: _____

Stress

Exercise Goals

Sleep   1   2   3   4   5   6   7   8+

Hydration

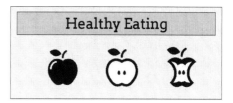

Healthy Eating

My riding goal for the day is: _____

_____

_____

_____

_____

My ride was: _____

_____

_____

_____

_____

_____

_____

Date: _____

Stress

Exercise Goals

Sleep   1   2   3   4   5   6   7   8+

Hydration

Healthy Eating

My riding goal for the day is:

_____

_____

_____

_____

My ride was: _____

_____

_____

_____

_____

_____

_____

I am most excited about this aspect of my riding:

_____

_____

_____

_____

_____

_____

_____

_____

_____

_____

_____

Date: _____

Stress

Exercise Goals

Sleep 1 2 3 4 5 6 7 8+

Hydration

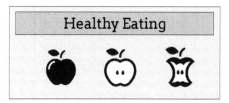
Healthy Eating

My riding goal for the day is: _____

_____

_____

_____

_____

My ride was: _____

_____

_____

_____

_____

_____

_____

Date: _____

Stress

Exercise Goals

Sleep   1 2 3 4 5 6 7 8+

Hydration

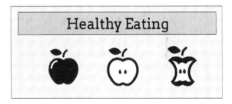

Healthy Eating

My riding goal for the day is: _____

_____

_____

_____

_____

My ride was: _____

_____

_____

_____

_____

_____

_____

_____

Date: _____

Stress

Exercise Goals

Sleep   1   2   3   4   5   6   7   8+

Hydration

Healthy Eating

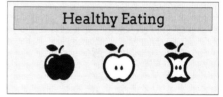

My riding goal for the day is: _____

_____

_____

_____

_____

My ride was: _____

_____

_____

_____

_____

_____

_____

_____

Date: _____

Stress

Exercise Goals

Sleep   1 2 3 4 5 6 7 8+

Hydration

Healthy Eating

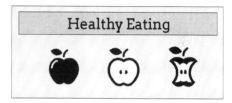

My riding goal for the day is: _____

_____

_____

_____

_____

My ride was: _____

_____

_____

_____

_____

_____

_____

_____

Date: _____

Stress

Exercise Goals

Sleep 1 2 3 4 5 6 7 8+

Hydration

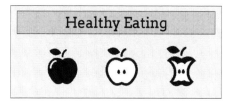
Healthy Eating

My riding goal for the day is: _____

_____

_____

_____

_____

My ride was: _____

_____

_____

_____

_____

_____

_____

Date: _____

Stress

Exercise Goals

Sleep   1 2 3 4 5 6 7 8+

Hydration

Healthy Eating

My riding goal for the day is:

_____

_____

_____

_____

My ride was: _____

_____

_____

_____

_____

_____

_____

How do you define your relationship with your horse?

_____

_____

_____

_____

_____

_____

_____

_____

_____

_____

_____

Date: _____

Stress

Exercise Goals

Sleep   1   2   3   4   5   6   7   8+

Hydration

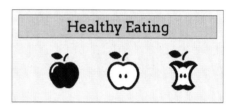
Healthy Eating

My riding goal for the day is: _____

_____

_____

_____

_____

My ride was: _____

_____

_____

_____

_____

_____

_____

_____

Date: _____

Stress

Exercise Goals

Sleep  1   2   3   4   5   6   7   8+

Hydration

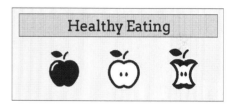

Healthy Eating

My riding goal for the day is: _____

_____

_____

_____

_____

My ride was: _____

_____

_____

_____

_____

_____

_____

_____

_____

Date: _____

Stress

Exercise Goals

Sleep   1   2   3   4   5   6   7   8+

Hydration

Healthy Eating

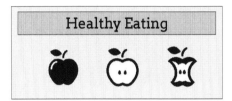

My riding goal for the day is: _____

_____

_____

_____

_____

My ride was: _____

_____

_____

_____

_____

_____

_____

Date: _____

Stress

Exercise Goals

Sleep   1   2   3   4   5   6   7   8+

Hydration

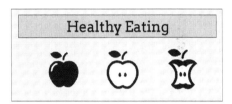
Healthy Eating

My riding goal for the day is: _____
_____
_____
_____
_____

My ride was: _____
_____
_____
_____
_____
_____
_____

Date: _____

Stress

Exercise Goals

Sleep   1   2   3   4   5   6   7   8+

Hydration

Healthy Eating

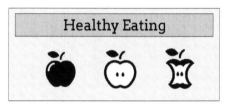

My riding goal for the day is: _____

_____

_____

_____

_____

My ride was: _____

_____

_____

_____

_____

_____

_____

_____

Date: _____

Stress

Exercise Goals

Sleep   1   2   3   4   5   6   7   8+

Hydration

Healthy Eating

My riding goal for the day is:

_____

_____

_____

_____

My ride was: _____

_____

_____

_____

_____

_____

_____

I will leave my stress behind today by:

_____

_____

_____

_____

_____

_____

_____

_____

_____

_____

_____

Date: _____

Stress

Exercise Goals

Sleep   1   2   3   4   5   6   7   8+

Hydration

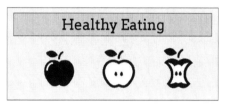
Healthy Eating

My riding goal for the day is: _____

_____

_____

_____

_____

My ride was: _____

_____

_____

_____

_____

_____

_____

_____

Date: _____

Stress

Exercise Goals

Sleep   1   2   3   4   5   6   7   8+

Hydration

Healthy Eating

My riding goal for the day is: _____

_____

_____

_____

_____

My ride was: _____

_____

_____

_____

_____

_____

_____

_____

Date: _____

Stress

Exercise Goals

Sleep   1   2   3   4   5   6   7   8+

Hydration

Healthy Eating

My riding goal for the day is: _____

_____

_____

_____

_____

My ride was: _____

_____

_____

_____

_____

_____

_____

Date: _____

Stress

Exercise Goals

Sleep   1   2   3   4   5   6   7   8+

Hydration

Healthy Eating

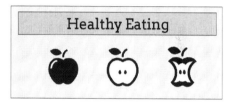

My riding goal for the day is: _____

_____

_____

_____

_____

My ride was: _____

_____

_____

_____

_____

_____

_____

_____

_____

Date: _____

Stress

Exercise Goals

Sleep 1 2 3 4 5 6 7 8+

Hydration

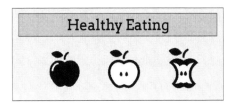

Healthy Eating

My riding goal for the day is: _____

_____

_____

_____

_____

My ride was: _____

_____

_____

_____

_____

_____

_____

Date: _____

Stress

Exercise Goals

Sleep   1   2   3   4   5   6   7   8+

Hydration

Healthy Eating

My riding goal for the day is:

_____

_____

_____

_____

My ride was: _____

_____

_____

_____

_____

_____

_____

How will you sense tension in your horse today? How will you help to manage that tension?

_____

_____

_____

_____

_____

_____

_____

_____

_____

_____

Date: _____

Stress

Exercise Goals

Sleep   1 2 3 4 5 6 7 8+

Hydration

Healthy Eating

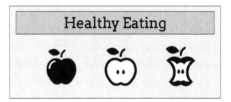

My riding goal for the day is: _____

_____

_____

_____

_____

My ride was: _____

_____

_____

_____

_____

_____

_____

Date: _____

Stress

Exercise Goals

Sleep 1   2   3   4   5   6   7   8+

Hydration

Healthy Eating

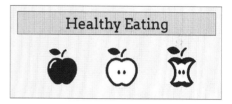

My riding goal for the day is: _____

_____

_____

_____

_____

My ride was: _____

_____

_____

_____

_____

_____

_____

_____

Date: _____

Stress

Exercise Goals

Sleep 　　1　　2　　3　　4　　5　　6　　7　　8+

Hydration

Healthy Eating

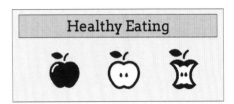

My riding goal for the day is: _____

_____

_____

_____

_____

My ride was: _____

_____

_____

_____

_____

_____

_____

Date: _____

Stress

Exercise Goals

Sleep 1   2   3   4   5   6   7   8+

Hydration

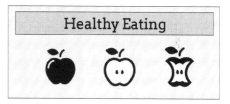

Healthy Eating

My riding goal for the day is: _____

_____

_____

_____

_____

My ride was: _____

_____

_____

_____

_____

_____

_____

_____

_____

Date: _____

Stress

Exercise Goals

Sleep 1 2 3 4 5 6 7 8+

Hydration

Healthy Eating

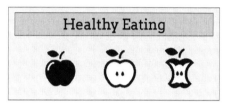

My riding goal for the day is: _____

_____

_____

_____

_____

My ride was: _____

_____

_____

_____

_____

_____

_____

Date: _____

Stress

Exercise Goals

Sleep   1 2 3 4 5 6 7 8+

Hydration

Healthy Eating

My riding goal for the day is:

_____

_____

_____

_____

My ride was: _____

_____

_____

_____

_____

_____

_____

When my horse makes a
mistake today, I will practice
kindness by:

_____

_____

_____

_____

_____

_____

_____

_____

_____

_____

Date: _____

Stress

Exercise Goals

Sleep   1   2   3   4   5   6   7   8+

Hydration

Healthy Eating

My riding goal for the day is: _____

_____

_____

_____

_____

My ride was: _____

_____

_____

_____

_____

_____

_____

Date: _____

Stress

Exercise Goals

Sleep   1   2   3   4   5   6   7   8+

Hydration

Healthy Eating

My riding goal for the day is: _____

_____

_____

_____

_____

My ride was: _____

_____

_____

_____

_____

_____

_____

Date: _____

Stress

Exercise Goals

Sleep   1   2   3   4   5   6   7   8+

Hydration

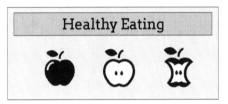

Healthy Eating

My riding goal for the day is: _____

_____

_____

_____

_____

My ride was: _____

_____

_____

_____

_____

_____

_____

Date: _____

Stress

Exercise Goals

Sleep   1   2   3   4   5   6   7   8+

Hydration

Healthy Eating

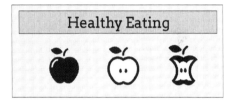

My riding goal for the day is: _____
_____
_____
_____
_____

My ride was: _____
_____
_____
_____
_____
_____
_____
_____

Stress

Exercise Goals

Sleep   1   2   3   4   5   6   7   8+

Hydration

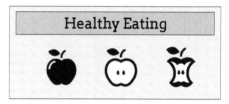

Healthy Eating

My riding goal for the day is: _____

_____

_____

_____

_____

My ride was: _____

_____

_____

_____

_____

_____

_____

_____

Date: _____

Stress

Exercise Goals

Sleep 1 2 3 4 5 6 7 8+

Hydration

Healthy Eating

My riding goal for the day is:

_____

_____

_____

_____

My ride was: _____

_____

_____

_____

_____

_____

_____

When I make a mistake today, I will practice kindness by:

_____

_____

_____

_____

_____

_____

_____

_____

_____

_____

Date: _____

Stress

Exercise Goals

Sleep 1 2 3 4 5 6 7 8+

Hydration

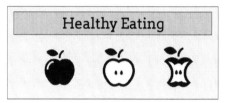
Healthy Eating

My riding goal for the day is: _____

_____

_____

_____

_____

My ride was: _____

_____

_____

_____

_____

_____

_____

Date: _____

Stress

Exercise Goals

Sleep   1   2   3   4   5   6   7   8+

Hydration

Healthy Eating

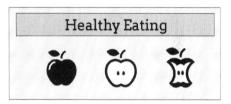

My riding goal for the day is: _____

_____

_____

_____

_____

My ride was: _____

_____

_____

_____

_____

_____

_____

_____

Date:_____

Stress

Exercise Goals

Sleep   1   2   3   4   5   6   7   8+

Hydration

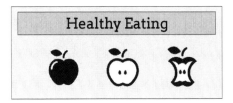

Healthy Eating

My riding goal for the day is: _____

_____

_____

_____

_____

My ride was: _____

_____

_____

_____

_____

_____

_____

Date: _____

Stress

Exercise Goals

Sleep   1   2   3   4   5   6   7   8+

Hydration

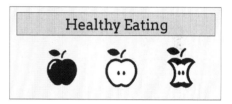

Healthy Eating

My riding goal for the day is: _____

_____

_____

_____

_____

My ride was: _____

_____

_____

_____

_____

_____

_____

_____

Date: _____

Stress

Sleep   1   2   3   4   5   6   7   8+

Hydration

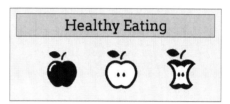

My riding goal for the day is: _____

_____

_____

_____

_____

My ride was: _____

_____

_____

_____

_____

_____

_____

_____

Date: _____

Stress

Exercise Goals

Sleep   1   2   3   4   5   6   7   8+

Hydration

Healthy Eating

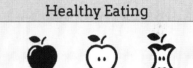

My riding goal for the day is:

_____

_____

_____

_____

My ride was: _____

_____

_____

_____

_____

_____

_____

How will you set aside time today to make sure you feel rested?

_____

_____

_____

_____

_____

_____

_____

_____

_____

_____

_____

Date: _____

Stress

Exercise Goals

Sleep 1 2 3 4 5 6 7 8+

Hydration

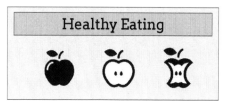

Healthy Eating

My riding goal for the day is: _____

_____

_____

_____

_____

My ride was: _____

_____

_____

_____

_____

_____

_____

Date: _____

Stress

Exercise Goals

Sleep 1 2 3 4 5 6 7 8+

Hydration

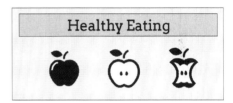

Healthy Eating

My riding goal for the day is: _____

_____

_____

_____

_____

My ride was: _____

_____

_____

_____

_____

_____

_____

Date: _____

Stress

Exercise Goals

Sleep   1   2   3   4   5   6   7   8+

Hydration

Healthy Eating

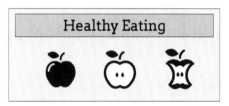

My riding goal for the day is: _____

_____

_____

_____

_____

My ride was: _____

_____

_____

_____

_____

_____

_____

_____

Date: _____

Stress

Exercise Goals

Sleep   1   2   3   4   5   6   7   8+

Hydration

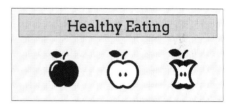
Healthy Eating

My riding goal for the day is: _____

_____

_____

_____

_____

My ride was: _____

_____

_____

_____

_____

_____

_____

_____

_____

Date: _____

Stress

Exercise Goals

Sleep   1   2   3   4   5   6   7   8+

Hydration

Healthy Eating

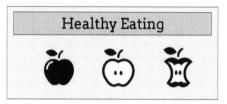

My riding goal for the day is: _____

_____

_____

_____

_____

My ride was: _____

_____

_____

_____

_____

_____

_____

Date: _____

Stress

Exercise Goals

Sleep 1 2 3 4 5 6 7 8+

Hydration

Healthy Eating

My riding goal for the day is:

_____

_____

_____

_____

My ride was: _____

_____

_____

_____

_____

_____

_____

At heart, my horse and I are:

_____

_____

_____

_____

_____

_____

_____

_____

_____

_____

_____

Date: _____

Stress

Exercise Goals

Sleep   1   2   3   4   5   6   7   8+

Hydration

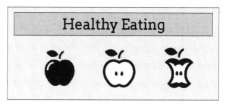
Healthy Eating

My riding goal for the day is: _____

_____

_____

_____

_____

My ride was: _____

_____

_____

_____

_____

_____

_____

Date: _____

Stress

Sleep   1   2   3   4   5   6   7   8+

Hydration

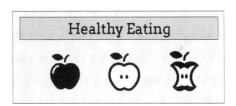

My riding goal for the day is: _____

_____

_____

_____

_____

My ride was: _____

_____

_____

_____

_____

_____

Date: _____

Stress

Exercise Goals

Sleep   1   2   3   4   5   6   7   8+

Hydration

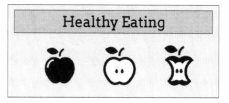

Healthy Eating

My riding goal for the day is: _____

_____

_____

_____

_____

My ride was: _____

_____

_____

_____

_____

_____

_____

_____

Date: _____

Stress

Exercise Goals

Sleep   1   2   3   4   5   6   7   8+

Hydration

Healthy Eating

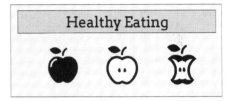

My riding goal for the day is: _____

_____

_____

_____

_____

My ride was: _____

_____

_____

_____

_____

_____

_____

Date: _____

Stress

Exercise Goals

Sleep   1   2   3   4   5   6   7   8+

Hydration

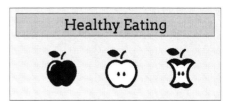

Healthy Eating

My riding goal for the day is: _____

_____

_____

_____

_____

My ride was: _____

_____

_____

_____

_____

_____

_____

_____

Date: _____

Stress

Exercise Goals

Sleep   1   2   3   4   5   6   7   8+

Hydration

Healthy Eating

My riding goal for the day is:

_____

_____

_____

_____

My ride was: _____

_____

_____

_____

_____

_____

_____

_____

What does it mean to be in a good rhythm when you ride? When you're not riding?

_____

_____

_____

_____

_____

_____

_____

_____

_____

_____

Date: _____

Stress

Sleep   1   2   3   4   5   6   7   8+

Hydration

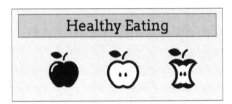

My riding goal for the day is: _____

_____

_____

_____

_____

My ride was: _____

_____

_____

_____

_____

_____

_____

Date: _____

Stress

Exercise Goals

Sleep 1 2 3 4 5 6 7 8+

Hydration

Healthy Eating

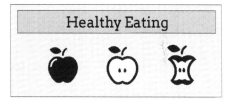

My riding goal for the day is: _____

_____

_____

_____

_____

My ride was: _____

_____

_____

_____

_____

_____

_____

_____

Date: _____

Stress

Exercise Goals

Sleep   1 2 3 4 5 6 7 8+

Hydration

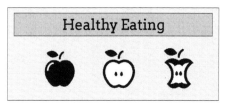

Healthy Eating

My riding goal for the day is: _____

_____

_____

_____

_____

My ride was: _____

_____

_____

_____

_____

_____

_____

_____

Date: _____

Stress

Sleep    1   2   3   4   5   6   7   8+

Hydration

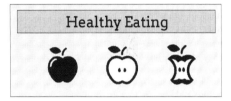

My riding goal for the day is: _____

_____

_____

_____

_____

My ride was: _____

_____

_____

_____

_____

_____

_____

Date: _____

Stress

Exercise Goals

Sleep   1   2   3   4   5   6   7   8+

Hydration

Healthy Eating

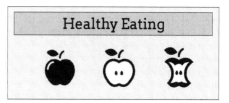

My riding goal for the day is: _____

_____

_____

_____

_____

My ride was: _____

_____

_____

_____

_____

_____

_____

Date: _____

Stress

Exercise Goals

Sleep   1   2   3   4   5   6   7   8+

Hydration

Healthy Eating

My riding goal for the day is:

_____

_____

_____

_____

My ride was: _____

_____

_____

_____

_____

_____

_____

How do you create relaxation in your horse? In yourself as you ride?

_____

_____

_____

_____

_____

_____

_____

_____

_____

_____

_____

Date: _____

Stress

Sleep   1   2   3   4   5   6   7   8+

Hydration

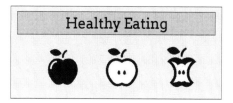

My riding goal for the day is: _____

_____

_____

_____

_____

My ride was: _____

_____

_____

_____

_____

_____

_____

_____

Date: _____

Stress

Exercise Goals

Sleep   1   2   3   4   5   6   7   8+

Hydration

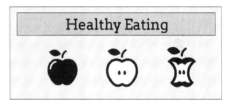

Healthy Eating

My riding goal for the day is: _____

_____

_____

_____

_____

My ride was: _____

_____

_____

_____

_____

_____

_____

_____

Date: _____

Stress

Exercise Goals

Sleep   1   2   3   4   5   6   7   8+

Hydration

Healthy Eating

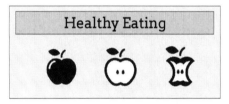

My riding goal for the day is: _____

_____

_____

_____

_____

My ride was: _____

_____

_____

_____

_____

_____

_____

_____

Date: _____

Stress

Sleep   1   2   3   4   5   6   7   8+

Hydration

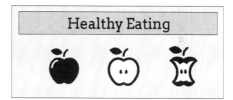

My riding goal for the day is: _____
_____
_____
_____
_____

My ride was: _____
_____
_____
_____
_____
_____
_____
_____
_____

Date: _____

Stress

Exercise Goals

Sleep   1   2   3   4   5   6   7   8+

Hydration

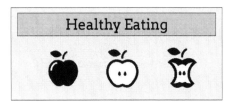

Healthy Eating

My riding goal for the day is: _____

_____

_____

_____

_____

My ride was: _____

_____

_____

_____

_____

_____

_____

Date: _____

Stress

Exercise Goals

Sleep   1   2   3   4   5   6   7   8+

Hydration

Healthy Eating

My riding goal for the day is:

_____

_____

_____

_____

My ride was: _____

_____

_____

_____

_____

_____

_____

If I feel overwhelmed today, I will:

_____

_____

_____

_____

_____

_____

_____

_____

_____

_____

_____

_____

Date: _____

Stress

Exercise Goals

Sleep   1   2   3   4   5   6   7   8+

Hydration

Healthy Eating

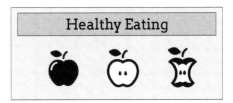

My riding goal for the day is: _____

_____

_____

_____

_____

My ride was: _____

_____

_____

_____

_____

_____

_____

Date: _____

Stress

Exercise Goals

Sleep   1   2   3   4   5   6   7   8+

Hydration

Healthy Eating

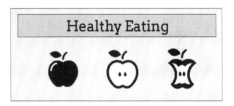

My riding goal for the day is: _____

_____

_____

_____

_____

My ride was: _____

_____

_____

_____

_____

_____

_____

Date: _____

Stress

Exercise Goals

Sleep   1   2   3   4   5   6   7   8+

Hydration

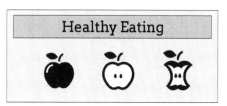

Healthy Eating

My riding goal for the day is: _____

_____

_____

_____

_____

My ride was: _____

_____

_____

_____

_____

_____

_____

Date: _____

Stress

Exercise Goals

Sleep   1 2 3 4 5 6 7 8+

Hydration

Healthy Eating

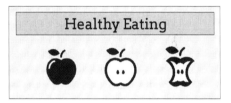

My riding goal for the day is: _____

_____

_____

_____

_____

My ride was: _____

_____

_____

_____

_____

_____

_____

Date: _____

Stress

Exercise Goals

Sleep   1   2   3   4   5   6   7   8+

Hydration

Healthy Eating

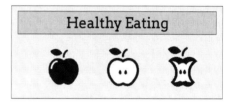

My riding goal for the day is: _____

_____

_____

_____

_____

My ride was: _____

_____

_____

_____

_____

_____

_____

_____

Date: _____

Stress

Sleep   1   2   3   4   5   6   7   8+

Hydration

My riding goal for the day is:

_____

_____

_____

_____

My ride was: _____

_____

_____

_____

_____

_____

_____

Take a moment and visualize the perfect ride. What is one small thing you can do to get closer to that vision?

_____

_____

_____

_____

_____

_____

_____

_____

_____

_____

Date: _____

Stress

Exercise Goals

Sleep   1   2   3   4   5   6   7   8+

Hydration

Healthy Eating

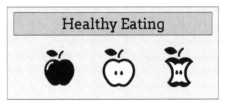

My riding goal for the day is: _____

_____

_____

_____

_____

My ride was: _____

_____

_____

_____

_____

_____

_____

Date: _____

Stress

Exercise Goals

Sleep 1 2 3 4 5 6 7 8+

Hydration

Healthy Eating

My riding goal for the day is: _____

_____

_____

_____

_____

My ride was: _____

_____

_____

_____

_____

_____

_____

Date: _____

Stress

Exercise Goals

Sleep   1   2   3   4   5   6   7   8+

Hydration

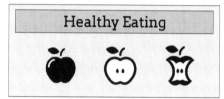

Healthy Eating

My riding goal for the day is: _____

_____

_____

_____

_____

My ride was: _____

_____

_____

_____

_____

_____

_____

_____

_____

Date: _____

Stress

Exercise Goals

Sleep 1 2 3 4 5 6 7 8+

Hydration

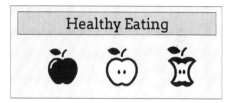

Healthy Eating

My riding goal for the day is: _____

_____

_____

_____

_____

My ride was: _____

_____

_____

_____

_____

_____

_____

_____

_____

Date: _____

Stress

Exercise Goals

Sleep   1   2   3   4   5   6   7   8+

Hydration

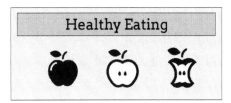

Healthy Eating

My riding goal for the day is: _____

_____

_____

_____

_____

My ride was: _____

_____

_____

_____

_____

_____

_____

Date: _____

Stress

Exercise Goals

Sleep   1   2   3   4   5   6   7   8+

Hydration

Healthy Eating

My riding goal for the day is:

_____

_____

_____

_____

My ride was: _____

_____

_____

_____

_____

_____

_____

What I have learned from all of my hard work is:

_____

_____

_____

_____

_____

_____

_____

_____

_____

_____

_____

_____

Date: _____

Stress

Exercise Goals

Sleep   1   2   3   4   5   6   7   8+

Hydration

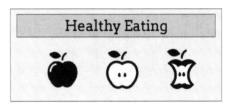

Healthy Eating

My riding goal for the day is: _____

_____

_____

_____

_____

My ride was: _____

_____

_____

_____

_____

_____

_____

Date: _____

Stress

Exercise Goals

Sleep   1   2   3   4   5   6   7   8+

Hydration

Healthy Eating

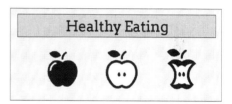

My riding goal for the day is: _____

_____

_____

_____

_____

My ride was: _____

_____

_____

_____

_____

_____

_____

_____

Date: _____

Stress

Exercise Goals

Sleep 1 2 3 4 5 6 7 8+

Hydration

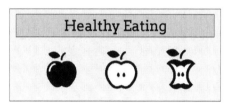
Healthy Eating

My riding goal for the day is: _____

_____

_____

_____

_____

My ride was: _____

_____

_____

_____

_____

_____

_____

Date: _____

Stress

Exercise Goals

Sleep  1 2 3 4 5 6 7 8+

Hydration

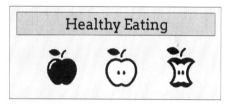
Healthy Eating

My riding goal for the day is: _____

_____

_____

_____

_____

My ride was: _____

_____

_____

_____

_____

_____

_____

_____

Date: _____

Stress

Exercise Goals

Sleep   1   2   3   4   5   6   7   8+

Hydration

Healthy Eating

My riding goal for the day is: _____

_____

_____

_____

_____

My ride was: _____

_____

_____

_____

_____

_____

_____

Date: _____

Stress

Exercise Goals

Sleep   1 2 3 4 5 6 7 8+

Hydration

Healthy Eating

My riding goal for the day is:

_____

_____

_____

My ride was: _____

_____

_____

_____

_____

_____

If something goes wrong in my ride, this is my strategy for staying positive:

_____

_____

_____

_____

_____

_____

_____

_____

_____

_____

Date: _____

Stress

Exercise Goals

Sleep   1   2   3   4   5   6   7   8+

Hydration

Healthy Eating

My riding goal for the day is: _____

_____

_____

_____

_____

My ride was: _____

_____

_____

_____

_____

_____

_____

_____

Date: _____

Stress

Exercise Goals

Sleep   1   2   3   4   5   6   7   8+

Hydration

Healthy Eating

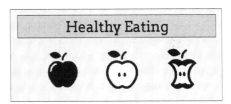

My riding goal for the day is: _____

_____

_____

_____

_____

My ride was: _____

_____

_____

_____

_____

_____

_____

Date: _____

Stress

Exercise Goals

Sleep   1   2   3   4   5   6   7   8+

Hydration

Healthy Eating

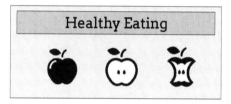

My riding goal for the day is: _____

_____

_____

_____

_____

My ride was: _____

_____

_____

_____

_____

_____

_____

_____

Date: _____

Stress

Exercise Goals

Sleep   1   2   3   4   5   6   7   8+

Hydration

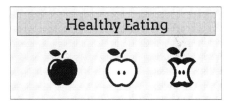
Healthy Eating

My riding goal for the day is: _____

_____

_____

_____

_____

My ride was: _____

_____

_____

_____

_____

_____

_____

_____

Date: _____

Stress

Exercise Goals

Sleep   1   2   3   4   5   6   7   8+

Hydration

Healthy Eating

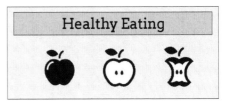

My riding goal for the day is: _____

_____

_____

_____

_____

My ride was: _____

_____

_____

_____

_____

_____

_____

Date: _____

Stress

Exercise Goals

Sleep 1 2 3 4 5 6 7 8+

Hydration

Healthy Eating

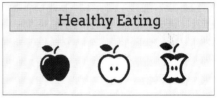

My riding goal for the day is:

_____

_____

_____

_____

My ride was: _____

_____

_____

_____

_____

_____

_____

Did you take better care of your horse than yourself today? If so, how could you help yourself to thrive?

_____

_____

_____

_____

_____

_____

_____

_____

_____

_____

_____

_____

Date: _____

Stress

Exercise Goals

Sleep   1   2   3   4   5   6   7   8+

Hydration

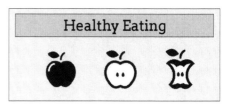
Healthy Eating

My riding goal for the day is: _____

_____

_____

_____

_____

My ride was: _____

_____

_____

_____

_____

_____

_____

Date: _____

Stress

Sleep   1   2   3   4   5   6   7   8+

Hydration

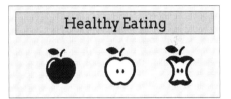

My riding goal for the day is: _____

_____

_____

_____

_____

My ride was: _____

_____

_____

_____

_____

_____

_____

Date: _____

Stress

Exercise Goals

Sleep   1   2   3   4   5   6   7   8+

Hydration

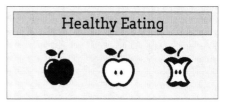

Healthy Eating

My riding goal for the day is: _____

_____

_____

_____

_____

My ride was: _____

_____

_____

_____

_____

_____

_____

_____

Date: _____

Stress

Exercise Goals

Sleep 1 2 3 4 5 6 7 8+

Hydration

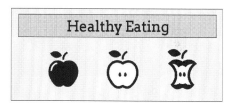

Healthy Eating

My riding goal for the day is: _____

_____

_____

_____

_____

My ride was: _____

_____

_____

_____

_____

_____

_____

_____

_____

Date: _____

Stress

Exercise Goals

Sleep 1 2 3 4 5 6 7 8+

Hydration

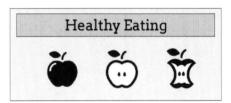

Healthy Eating

My riding goal for the day is: _____

_____

_____

_____

_____

My ride was: _____

_____

_____

_____

_____

_____

_____

_____

Date: _____

Stress

Exercise Goals

Sleep 1 2 3 4 5 6 7 8+

Hydration

Healthy Eating

My riding goal for the day is:

_____

_____

_____

_____

My ride was: _____

_____

_____

_____

_____

_____

_____

When are you and your horse at your most powerful? How do you get there?

_____

_____

_____

_____

_____

_____

_____

_____

_____

_____

Date: _____

Stress

Exercise Goals

Sleep   1   2   3   4   5   6   7   8+

Hydration

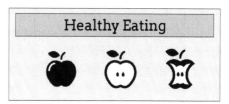

Healthy Eating

My riding goal for the day is: _____

_____

_____

_____

_____

My ride was: _____

_____

_____

_____

_____

_____

_____

Date: _____

Stress

Exercise Goals

Sleep   1 2 3 4 5 6 7 8+

Hydration

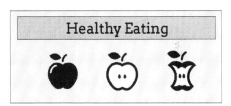

Healthy Eating

My riding goal for the day is: _____

_____

_____

_____

_____

My ride was: _____

_____

_____

_____

_____

_____

_____

Date:_____

Stress

Exercise Goals

Sleep   1   2   3   4   5   6   7   8+

Hydration

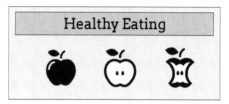

Healthy Eating

My riding goal for the day is: _____

_____

_____

_____

_____

My ride was: _____

_____

_____

_____

_____

_____

_____

Date: _____

Stress

Sleep   1   2   3   4   5   6   7   8+

Hydration

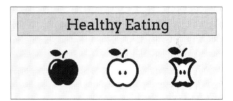

My riding goal for the day is: _____

_____

_____

_____

_____

My ride was: _____

_____

_____

_____

_____

_____

_____

Stress

Exercise Goals

Sleep 1　　2　　3　　4　　5　　6　　7　　8+

Hydration

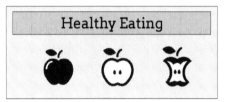

Healthy Eating

My riding goal for the day is: _____

_____

_____

_____

_____

My ride was: _____

_____

_____

_____

_____

_____

_____

Date: _____

Stress

Exercise Goals

Sleep 1 2 3 4 5 6 7 8+

Hydration

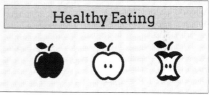

Healthy Eating

My riding goal for the day is:

_____

_____

_____

_____

My ride was: _____

_____

_____

_____

_____

_____

_____

Today I will practice centred riding by:

_____

_____

_____

_____

_____

_____

_____

_____

_____

_____

_____

_____

Date: _____

Stress

Sleep   1   2   3   4   5   6   7   8+

Hydration

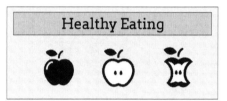

My riding goal for the day is: _____

_____

_____

_____

_____

My ride was: _____

_____

_____

_____

_____

_____

_____

Date: _____

Stress

Sleep   1   2   3   4   5   6   7   8+

Hydration

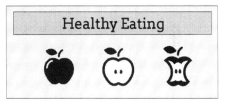

My riding goal for the day is: _____

_____

_____

_____

_____

My ride was: _____

_____

_____

_____

_____

_____

_____

_____

Date:_____

Stress

Exercise Goals

Sleep 1 2 3 4 5 6 7 8+

Hydration

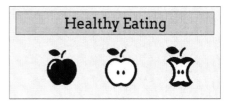

Healthy Eating

My riding goal for the day is: _____

_____

_____

_____

_____

My ride was: _____

_____

_____

_____

_____

_____

_____

Date: _____

Stress

Exercise Goals

Sleep   1   2   3   4   5   6   7   8+

Hydration

Healthy Eating

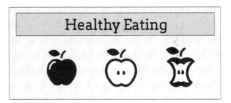

My riding goal for the day is: _____

_____

_____

_____

_____

My ride was: _____

_____

_____

_____

_____

_____

Date: _____

Stress

Exercise Goals

Sleep   1   2   3   4   5   6   7   8+

Hydration

Healthy Eating

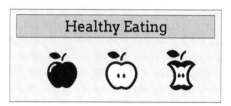

My riding goal for the day is: _____

_____

_____

_____

_____

My ride was: _____

_____

_____

_____

_____

_____

_____

_____

Date: _____

Stress

Exercise Goals

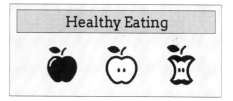

Sleep   1   2   3   4   5   6   7   8+

Hydration

Healthy Eating

My riding goal for the day is:

_____

_____

_____

_____

My ride was: _____

_____

_____

_____

_____

_____

_____

This is why I trust my horse:

_____

_____

_____

_____

_____

_____

_____

_____

_____

_____

_____

Date: _____

Stress

Exercise Goals

Sleep   1   2   3   4   5   6   7   8+

Hydration

Healthy Eating

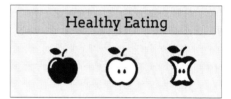

My riding goal for the day is: _____

_____

_____

_____

_____

My ride was: _____

_____

_____

_____

_____

_____

_____

_____

Stress

Exercise Goals

Sleep   1   2   3   4   5   6   7   8+

Hydration

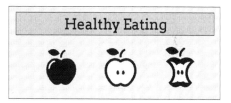

Healthy Eating

My riding goal for the day is: _____

_____

_____

_____

_____

My ride was: _____

_____

_____

_____

_____

_____

_____

_____

Date: _____

Stress

Exercise Goals

Sleep   1   2   3   4   5   6   7   8+

Hydration

Healthy Eating

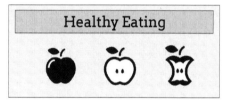

My riding goal for the day is: _____

_____

_____

_____

_____

My ride was: _____

_____

_____

_____

_____

_____

_____

Date: _____

Stress

Exercise Goals

Sleep   1   2   3   4   5   6   7   8+

Hydration

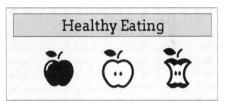

Healthy Eating

My riding goal for the day is: _____

_____

_____

_____

_____

My ride was: _____

_____

_____

_____

_____

_____

_____

_____

Date:_____

Stress

Sleep 1   2   3   4   5   6   7   8+

Hydration

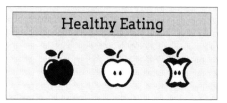

My riding goal for the day is: _____

_____

_____

_____

_____

My ride was: _____

_____

_____

_____

_____

_____

_____

Date: _____

Stress

Exercise Goals

Sleep   1   2   3   4   5   6   7   8+

Hydration

Healthy Eating

My riding goal for the day is:

_____

_____

_____

_____

My ride was: _____

_____

_____

_____

_____

_____

_____

My horse and I make the best team because:

_____

_____

_____

_____

_____

_____

_____

_____

_____

_____

_____

_____

Date: _____

Stress

Exercise Goals

Sleep 1 2 3 4 5 6 7 8+

Hydration

Healthy Eating

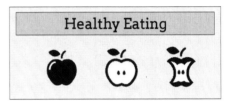

My riding goal for the day is: _____

_____

_____

_____

_____

My ride was: _____

_____

_____

_____

_____

_____

_____

_____

Stress

Exercise Goals

Sleep   1 2 3 4 5 6 7 8+

Hydration

Healthy Eating

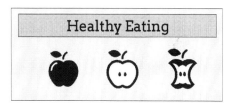

My riding goal for the day is: _____

_____

_____

_____

_____

My ride was: _____

_____

_____

_____

_____

_____

_____

_____

_____

Date: _____

Stress

Exercise Goals

Sleep   1   2   3   4   5   6   7   8+

Hydration

Healthy Eating

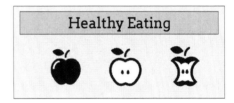

My riding goal for the day is: _____

_____

_____

_____

_____

My ride was: _____

_____

_____

_____

_____

_____

_____

Date: _____

Stress

Exercise Goals

Sleep 1   2   3   4   5   6   7   8+

Hydration

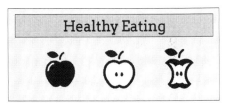

Healthy Eating

My riding goal for the day is: _____

_____

_____

_____

_____

My ride was: _____

_____

_____

_____

_____

_____

_____

_____

Date: _____

Stress

Exercise Goals

Sleep 1 2 3 4 5 6 7 8+

Hydration

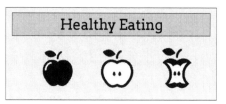

Healthy Eating

My riding goal for the day is: _____

_____

_____

_____

_____

My ride was: _____

_____

_____

_____

_____

_____

_____

_____

Date: _____

Stress

Exercise Goals

Sleep   1   2   3   4   5   6   7   8+

Hydration

Healthy Eating

My riding goal for the day is:

_____

_____

_____

_____

My ride was: ———————————

_____

_____

_____

_____

_____

_____

I'm proudest of my horse and I for improving at:

_____

_____

_____

_____

_____

_____

_____

_____

_____

_____

_____

_____

_____

Date:_____

Stress

Exercise Goals

Sleep   1   2   3   4   5   6   7   8+

Hydration

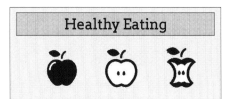

Healthy Eating

My riding goal for the day is: _____

_____

_____

_____

_____

My ride was: _____

_____

_____

_____

_____

_____

_____

_____

Date: _____

Stress

Exercise Goals

Sleep   1   2   3   4   5   6   7   8+

Hydration

Healthy Eating

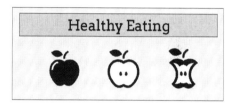

My riding goal for the day is: _____

_____

_____

_____

_____

My ride was: _____

_____

_____

_____

_____

_____

_____

_____

Date: _____

Stress

Sleep   1   2   3   4   5   6   7   8+

Hydration

Healthy Eating

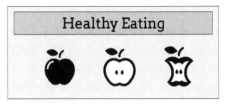

My riding goal for the day is: _____

_____

_____

_____

_____

My ride was: _____

_____

_____

_____

_____

_____

_____

_____

Date: _____

Stress

Exercise Goals

Sleep   1   2   3   4   5   6   7   8+

Hydration

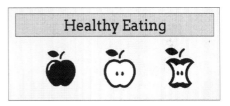

Healthy Eating

My riding goal for the day is: _____
_____
_____
_____
_____

My ride was: _____
_____
_____
_____
_____
_____
_____

Date: _____

Stress

Exercise Goals

Sleep   1 2 3 4 5 6 7 8+

Hydration

Healthy Eating

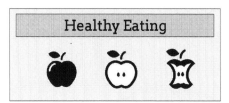

My riding goal for the day is: _____

_____

_____

_____

_____

My ride was: _____

_____

_____

_____

_____

_____

_____

_____

_____

Date: _____

Stress

Exercise Goals

Sleep   1   2   3   4   5   6   7   8+

Hydration

Healthy Eating

My riding goal for the day is:

_____

_____

_____

_____

My ride was: _____

_____

_____

_____

_____

_____

_____

This is the quality I most embody as a rider:

_____

_____

_____

_____

_____

_____

_____

_____

_____

_____

_____

_____

Date: _____

Stress

Exercise Goals

Sleep   1   2   3   4   5   6   7   8+

Hydration

Healthy Eating

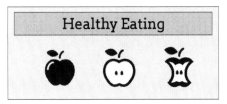

My riding goal for the day is: _____

_____

_____

_____

_____

My ride was: _____

_____

_____

_____

_____

_____

_____

_____

Stress

Sleep 1 2 3 4 5 6 7 8+

Hydration

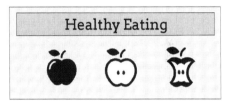

My riding goal for the day is: _____

_____

_____

_____

_____

My ride was: _____

_____

_____

_____

_____

_____

_____

Date: _____

Stress

Exercise Goals

Sleep   1 2 3 4 5 6 7 8+

Hydration

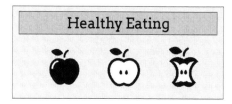

Healthy Eating

My riding goal for the day is: _____

_____

_____

_____

_____

My ride was: _____

_____

_____

_____

_____

_____

_____

Date: _____

Stress

Exercise Goals

Sleep 1 2 3 4 5 6 7 8+

Hydration

Healthy Eating

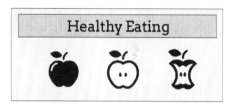

My riding goal for the day is: _____

_____

_____

_____

_____

My ride was: _____

_____

_____

_____

_____

_____

_____

_____

_____

Date: _____

Stress

Exercise Goals

Sleep   1   2   3   4   5   6   7   8+

Hydration

Healthy Eating

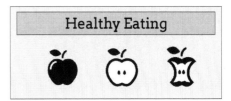

My riding goal for the day is: _____

_____

_____

_____

_____

My ride was: _____

_____

_____

_____

_____

_____

_____

_____

Date: _____

Stress

Exercise Goals

Sleep   1   2   3   4   5   6   7   8+

Hydration

Healthy Eating

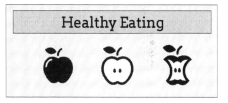

My riding goal for the day is:

_____

_____

_____

_____

My ride was: ——————————

_____

_____

_____

_____

_____

_____

I can keep this image in my mind to find harmony with my horse:

_____

_____

_____

_____

_____

_____

_____

_____

_____

_____

_____

Date: _____

Stress

Exercise Goals

Sleep   1   2   3   4   5   6   7   8+

Hydration

Healthy Eating

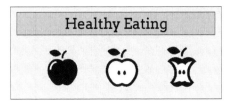

My riding goal for the day is: _____

_____

_____

_____

_____

My ride was: _____

_____

_____

_____

_____

_____

_____

Date: _____

Stress

Sleep   1 2 3 4 5 6 7 8+

Hydration

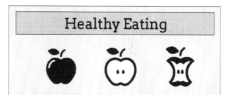

My riding goal for the day is: _____

_____

_____

_____

_____

My ride was: _____

_____

_____

_____

_____

_____

_____

_____

Journaling Prompts

1. Riding makes me feel:

2. Take a moment and describe the partnership you have with your horse.

3. How can you be more present for your horse when you ride?

4. I feel most alive when I'm:

5. Today I was challenged by:

6. When my horse and I are really connected, it feels:

7. My horse and I are most together when:

8. This is how I will banish negative thoughts today:

9. Take a moment and just breathe together with your horse. How does that affect your riding?

10. I feel most at home in the saddle when I'm:

11. The strongest thing about my riding today was:

12. Today I will:

13. This is what makes me trust in myself:

14. I love it when my horse:

15. What have you been avoiding in your riding? How will you confront it?

16. I will work to stay open to new experiences by:

17. How will you take extra good care of your body today?

18. What did you expect of your ride today? Where did those expectations come from?

19. Today, I will create the ride I want by:

20. This is what makes me believe in my horse:

21. I will overcome fear today by:

22. This is my expression of faith in myself.

22. I will show my appreciation for my horse today by:

23. I will show my appreciation for myself today by:

24. Today, I will celebrate:

25. How will you embody kindness today?

26. This is what helps me be my best:

27. What is your horse's greatest strength?

28. When did you and your horse start your journey together? Where do you hope it goes?

29. Concentrate on how it feels to be truly centered in the saddle. How do you find that feeling?

30. This is what helps my horse be her/his best:

31. Today I am grateful for:

32. I feel most free when I:

33. How will you connect your mind and your body as you ride?

34. What helps you to focus when you're riding?

35. I admire the way my horse and I:

36. Who helps you to ride your very best? How can you say thank-you?

37. My horse enjoys herself/himself most when we:

38. For me, balance is:

39. How will you nurture your and your horse's emotional well-being during your ride today?

40. I will practice good self-care in the saddle by:

41. What is your attitude towards your riding today? How is it impacting your riding?

42. I am strongest when I:

43. This is how my horse helps me to be a better person:

44. This is how I help my horse be a better horse:

45. What role does riding play in keeping you balanced in your life?

46. What do you most need to stop thinking about so you can concentrate on your ride? How will you put those thoughts away?

47. This is how I plan to share a connection with my horse today:

48. This is what I need to give my best today:

49. How will you find peace in the saddle today?

50. I am most excited about this aspect of my riding:

51. How do you define your relationship with your horse?

52. I will leave my stress behind today by:

53. How will you sense tension in your horse today? How will you help to manage that tension?

54. When my horse makes a mistake today, I will practice kindness by:

55. When I make a mistake today, I will practice kindness by:

56. How will you set aside time today to make sure you feel rested?

57. At heart, my horse and I are:

58. What does it mean to be in a good rhythm when you ride? When you're not riding?

59. My horse and I can achieve balance by:

60. How do you create relaxation in your horse? In yourself as you ride?

61. If I feel overwhelmed today, I will:

62. Take a moment and visualize the perfect ride. What is one small thing you can do to get closer to that vision?

63. What I have learned from all of my hard work is:

64. If something goes wrong in my ride, this is my strategy for staying positive:

65. Did you take better care of your horse than yourself today? If so, how could you help yourself to thrive?

66. When are you and your horse at your most powerful? How do you get there?

67. Today I will practice centred riding by:

68. This is why I trust my horse:

69. My horse and I make the best team because:

70. I'm proudest of my horse and I for improving at:

71. This is the quality I most embody as a rider:

72. I can keep this image in my mind to find harmony with my horse:

Competitions

"He knows when you're happy. He knows when you're comfortable. He knows when you're confident. And he always knows when you have carrots."

Show Checklist

For the Horse

- ☐ Equine First Aid Kit
- ☐ Hay and Hay Net
- ☐ Water Buckets, Clips and Jugs of Water
- ☐ Feed and Supplements
- ☐ Halter, Lead Rope, Lunge Line
- ☐ Back up Halter, Lead Rope, Lunge Line
- ☐ Tack and Back up Tack
- ☐ Tack Cleaning Supplies
- ☐ Wraps and Boots (regular and shipping)
- ☐ Cooler and/or Sheet
- ☐ Grooming Supplies and Towels
- ☐ Bath Supplies
- ☐ Fly Spray
- ☐ Braiding Kit and Scissors
- ☐ Lots of Treats

For/From the Show Office

- ☐ Association Memberships
- ☐ Horse Passport
- ☐ Registration Papers
- ☐ Negative Coggins and/or Other Required Health Documentation
- ☐ Rulebook
- ☐ Cash or Cheque Book
- ☐ Copy of Tests, Patterns and Class Lists

For the Rider

- ☐ Rider Health Card
- ☐ Human First Aid Kit
- ☐ Sunscreen and Sun Protection
- ☐ Water
- ☐ Helmet
- ☐ Show Clothes and Safety Vest
- ☐ Cover-up Clothes for Grooming
- ☐ Gloves
- ☐ Rain Gear
- ☐ Safety Pins, Sewing Kit, Spot Cleaner
- ☐ Folding Chairs
- ☐ Cell Phone and List of Emergency Numbers
- ☐ Watch

For the Trailer

- ☐ Safety Check
- ☐ Spare Tire and Jack
- ☐ Extra Ties
- ☐ Hay Nets and Hay
- ☐ Bedding
- ☐ Muck Bucket and Forks
- ☐ Duct Tape, Flashlight

Journaling Prompts for Show Days

If your nerves start to get to you on a competition day, use these prompts to ground yourself and find focus again.

Today, this is the feeling I want to have with my horse: _____

_____

_____

_____

_____

_____

This is one failsafe thing I can do to find that feeling: _____

_____

_____

_____

_____

This is how I plan to manage distractions and stay focused on the present:

_____

_____

_____

_____

This is how I will take good care of my body on show day: _____

_____

_____

_____

_____

Today I will nurture my horse's body by: _____

_____

_____

_____

_____

In every situation, I will use this phrase or image to remind me that I choose my responses:

_____

_____

_____

_____

_____

I will practice gratitude and kindness at the competition by: _____

_____

_____

_____

_____

This is my affirmation of faith in my horse and in myself: _____

_____

_____

_____

_____

Show Log

Date	Venue/Series	Judge	Class	Placing	Number	Points

Date	Venue/Series	Judge	Class	Placing	Number	Points

Show Log

Date	Venue/Series	Judge	Class	Placing	Number	Points

Date	Venue/Series	Judge	Class	Placing	Number	Points

Show Log

Date	Venue/ Series	Judge	Class	Placing	Number	Points

Date	Venue/Series	Judge	Class	Placing	Number	Points

Notes

"The horse. Here is nobility without conceit, friendship without envy, beauty without vanity. A willing servant, yet never a slave."

RONALD DUNCAN

"I've spent most of my life riding horses. The rest I've just wasted."

"A true horseman does not look at the horse with his eyes,
he looks at his horse with his heart."

"To ride on a horse is to fly without wings."

"No heaven can heaven be, if my horse isn't there to welcome me."

MORE BOOKS BY

THE FARRIER GUIDE

Visit Our Book Store at thefarrierguide.com

HORSE OWNER JOURNAL

Track horse health, log farrier and vet visits, keep track of farm expenses --everything you need to record, all in one place!

List Price: $12.95
8.5" x 11" (21.59 x 27.94 cm)
110 pages
ISBN-13: 978-1988245362

HORSE OWNER JOURNAL
(Barn Edition)

Keep records for one year for up to twenty horses. Stay organized and take great care of your equine partners with this journal.

List Price: $19.95
8.5" x 11" (21.59 x 27.94 cm)
300 pages
ISBN-13: 978-1988245621

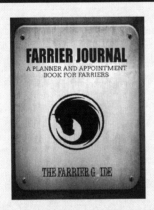

FARRIER JOURNAL

Finally, a day planner designed just for farriers. Functional, multi-purpose organizer keeps everything you need in one place!

List Price: $17.95
8.5" x 11" (21.59 x 27.94 cm)
378 pages
ISBN-13: 978-1987869729

THE FARRIER GUIDE

Learn all about farriery, horses, equine science and horse careers by reading our informative guides and articles and keeping in touch with our monthly newsletter and social media pages.

Visit us online at
www.thefarrierguide.com

77773448R00239

Made in the USA
Middletown, DE
25 June 2018